generations
of
edibles

a Southern Legacy

Peanut Butter Cookies

shortening — 1 c. white sugar — 2 well beaten

...salt... cup Peanut...

...Peanut butter, 1 T. milk

...shortening...

Fruit Cake Cookies

6 c. pecans
3 c. sifted
1 t. cinnamon
1 t. nutmeg
1 t. soda
1 c. liquid

...fruit and nuts. Combine
...pound...nut. Mix.
Well — add 2 c. flour & eggs

...remaining ingredients
mix well & sift flour

Corn Bread

Beat 4 eggs
Bake — 2 cups butter
1 tsp soda
2 cups corn meal
1 tsp. salt
grease pan Bake
min at 45...

Lime Salad
make jello — congeal
slightly mix with
...of cream cheese

generations of edibles

a Southern Legacy

a cookbook by elizabeth h. weaver

color photography by keith goodwin

I could start this welcome by saying food has always been an important part of my life. Then again, we could all say that, right? We need food to survive and survival is important. For me, food means family, friends, gatherings, traditions and typically fun. The reading of ingredients, the original form of a recipe, evokes a strong love of family recipes for me. All I've ever wanted from any family member who has decided to "leave" me something are things related to the meals: we have shared cast iron pans, recipes and magic secrets to producing their dish.

I have always had family members around me who could cook. Not just the women but also the men in my family can hold their own in the kitchen. My earliest memories of my MaMa (my paternal great-grandmother) are of her in the kitchen. I remember her most as a baker who used a tea cup for measuring and her demand for flour to be the White Lily Flour. My Nanny, (my maternal grandmother) was also a great baker, but that's not all. She could master any task she decided to conquer. Nanny was a brilliant math teacher, and every recipe has pencil markings changing measurements and "math-ing" things out the way she knew they would turn out best.

Grandmother and Granddaddy Hodges brought sophistication to my food memories. My first "fancy" meals were with them. The Christmas Eve table was always beautifully dressed as were the guests with good manners, beef tenderloin, elegant appetizers and ice cream cone clowns for the grandchildren that could only come from Baskin Robbins! I vacationed with these two quite often, and that meant at least one or two nights out in restaurants with amazing food choices. I can remember taking delicious cinnamon rolls home for breakfast the next morning or recreating a salad I'd enjoyed while out with them at an upscale restaurant, but these two could be happy at a

hole in the wall. Granddaddy loved to sneak a bite from Grandmother's plate. That was NOT proper in her opinion! It cracked me up whenever it happened because otherwise they were always very proper.

For Christmas one year my Grandmother Hodges gave each granddaughter a metal recipe box with all of her favorite recipes handwritten on cards. This is my greatest recipe treasure! I love and have even laughed at the recipes. My dad and I quickly learned that these recipes were not perfect as written. We've discovered some ingredients are missing and in several instances the ingredients are written with the brand name versus the actual name of the kind of ingredient. God bless the internet! Nevertheless, these recipes represent a period in time. The techniques are different and have evolved or fallen away over the years. The types of food served and the way they were served have gone by the way side in some cases. As I worked through them I realized many of these techniques and styles could (and should) be part of our everyday food practices. I use them now when I cook as well as when I teach.

You will find many pies, pound cakes and casserole variations in this cookbook. They all have a place in my food life. Sometimes food needs are based on time and place. Often, a meal is based on what we have on hand and how quickly the dishes need to appear. I am a great believer in maintaining a well-stocked pantry.

During the last years I worked for Cobb County Government in the Cultural Affairs Division, I realized that I would not retire and just sit around eating bon-bons. I don't "sit" well anyway. I had choices. It boiled down to two; professional theatrical directing or cooking. As I researched the cooking option I discovered a wonderful group of chefs who call themselves Personal Chefs. The more I read about this type of chef-work the more I knew it was for me. Preparing meals every week for families, making a lovely meal happen for a dinner party or handling food for large events was like taking all of my directing talents and producing broccoli and steak as the actors instead of people. Either way there is applause in some form at the end.

Generation of Edibles is not just about the generations who preceded me. Cooking for me began as a way to help around the house in my early teens. In college, it was a way to eat for less and to create items better than ramen noodles. When I was working in the arts, cooking became a stress reliever as well as a way to entertain. No matter what happened during the day, I could go into the kitchen with a list of ingredients and tame them into something that made me and others happy. You might call creating food for others the Curtain Call of the food world. I love taking that bow.

For the last 6 years I have been fortunate enough to work as a Personal Chef. It has been the most God-driven thing I have ever done. My husband helps me at every turn, my children and even grandchildren have helped with events. I see my food-love continuing on into the following generations as my legacy to them.

Treasure your own generations of edibles. Sit back and think what has impacted your food world. You can probably pick up an apple and smell a pie baking or see a chicken leg and remember when that was the only piece of fried chicken left for you to eat at Sunday dinner. Maybe your food memories need to be increased. If so, start today. Try new things or recreate something old. I always say if you can read you can cook. You must be able to read; so put on an apron and head to the kitchen! You have a generations who came before you. Honor their memories and you have generations that will come after you. Show them your love and love for food by creating and writing it all down!

happiness

My Nanny placed this lovely recipe in the Barnesville Baptist Cookbook. All of these ingredients help bring happiness. For me, there is a sixth ingredient, cooking for others. That always makes me happy.

2 heaping cups of patience

1 heart full of love

2 handfuls generosity

A dash of laughter

1 headful of understanding

Sprinkle generously with kindness; add plenty of faith and mix well. Spread over a period of a lifetime and serve to everybody you meet.

At first or second glance Elizabeth Weaver's Generations of Edibles: A Southern Legacy may seem to be "just" another cookbook. Yes, it has ingredient lists and assembly directions like any good cookbook, but take a minute to delve into the book's contents and you'll discover it is really a love letter.

Generations of Edibles: A Southern Legacy is an expression of Elizabeth's love of family, of tradition, of the gathering of friends or of feeding a crowd at an event. She perceptively recognized early in life that people must eat to live, but a simple (or glorious) meal shared with another will feed not only the body, but also the heart and soul.

In the South we have a lot of "sayin's." Not surprisingly, many of them have to do with food: e.g. "Food is love. Love is food. It's all good;" "Worries go down better with soup," and "A real Southern girl should own an iced tea pitcher and a deviled egg plate." The list goes on and on, but enjoying a snack or a meal with others proves the truth of the expression," Good food ends with good talk." Why, even at a planning session for a bridal or baby shower food is eaten and enjoyed while the menu for the event is discussed.

The telling of favorite family stories around the table is a time- honored tradition. Enjoying the favorite dishes of loved ones who are now absent from the table helps keep their memories alive as well as spark the remembrance of some long-forgotten tale that needs to be retold.

One of Elizabeth's many talents is the ability to instill confidence in others. I have personally experienced this phenomenon over and over. Because she believed I could do something I would think to myself, "Well, Elizabeth thinks I can; so, I must be able to," and I would do it!

Also counted among her gifts is problem solving. She has a way of breaking a task down into easy-to-accomplish steps; therefore, Generations of Edibles: A Southern Legacy has each recipe carefully crafted in order for you to recreate these delicious dishes with no frustration or missteps on your part.

If food is love, surely cooking is love made visible! Standing alone at Elizabeth's kitchen counter is a stool. It has been dubbed "the chair of truth," and countless family members and friends have taken turns sitting in it to pour out their hearts, to laugh or to gain some bit of wisdom--all while watching Elizabeth make her love for them manifest.

In her perfect world Elizabeth would personally cook for and serve you, but this is far from a perfect world! So, she has done the next best thing and made it possible for you to make love visible to your own family and friends with this far-from-ordinary cookbook.

For nearly thirty years Elizabeth Weaver and I have been friends. Despite a considerable age-gap, our strong faith in God, as well as our mutual love of musical theatre and oh-so-many other interests bonded our hearts.

It is my great privilege to invite you to leaf through the pages of Generations of Edibles: A Southern Legacy with the notion that it is a loving homage to the great Southern cooks who have surrounded Elizabeth all of her life, and a simple love letter to inspire you to think about what type of legacy you will leave for those who will follow in your footsteps.

As I often say, "It's never too late to start a new tradition!"

Carol V. Aebersold
Co-author of The Elf on the Shelf: A Christmas Tradition

table of contents

a Southern Legacy

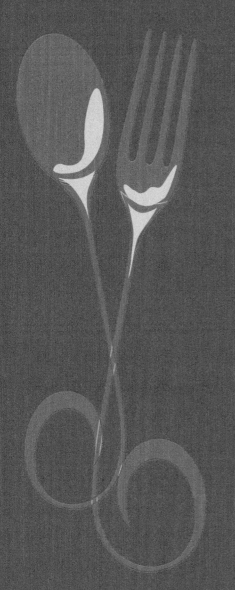

breakfast anytime

john's bloody mary

Christmas morning for decades has included this drink. John, my brother, created it and my Dad perfected it. Even those people who say they do not like tomato juice will enjoy John's Bloody Mary. I think what makes this drink great is the fresh lime juice. My Dad always serves it virgin and let's you add your vodka as you see fit. This drink is not typically dangerous on Christmas morning unless someone is late and this makes breakfast late. That gives us way too much time to drink.

32 ounce can Campbell's, low sodium tomato juice

4 ounces vodka

3 tablespoons Worcestershire sauce

1 teaspoon sugar

1 teaspoon salt

Juice of 6 limes

Hot sauce - optional

1. Pretty simple. **Mix in a large pitcher and chill.**
2. Vodka can be omitted and added as desired by each guest.

grandmother's cheese grits

It's not possible to have the Hodges' Christmas morning buffet without this dish.
It is a recipe I treasure. My grandmother always made this cheese grits casserole.
For many years she would make extra so that we could take some home with us.
One Christmas Grandmother shared her recipe with everyone in the family.   My Dad and I
made the grits years later and realized the recipe needed a little tweaking to recreate her exact
version. I believe we finally have it perfected. It is wonderful for feeding a crowd because it re-
ally does make a gracious amount. It is very important not to use instant grits.
You will want to use stone ground grits to achieve the best results.
The recipe freezes beautifully so you can prepare it ahead and bake when ready.

5 cups boiling water

1 1/2 cups regular grits (not instant),
preferably stone ground

1/2 cup butter

1/2 cup milk

1 pound sharp cheddar cheese, grated

2 teaspoons salt

3 large eggs, beaten

1/4 teaspoon black pepper

1/4 teaspoon Worcestershire sauce

1. **Preheat oven to 325 degrees.**
2. **Cook grits** in boiling water (stone ground grits, not quick/instant grits) for 10 - 12 minutes.
3. **Remove** from heat. **Add** the butter, salt, milk and cheese. **Mix** well. When slightly cooled **add beaten eggs, pepper and Worcestershire sauce**. Mix well. Put the mixture in a well greased 9 x 13 casserole dish. If you are not freezing the casserole, skip step 4.
4. **Cover** well with plastic wrap and foil. **Label and date** this dish. **Freeze** before cooking. Let **thaw overnight** before baking.
5. **Bake for 1 1/2 hours and serve**. This reheating very well in the microwave.

curried baked fruit

I remember this dish from many brunch gatherings with my Grandmother Hodges. It has a distinct aroma due to the curry and fruit juices. Eating curried fruit was my first experience with curry. It was a flavor unlike anything I had tried before. I can not say as a child that I ate a big serving, but I tasted it. I have learned as an adult it is a wonderful side dish. I really like this during the winter months. The warm fruits with the curry add such a unique touch as a side dish. You can make this with canned or fresh fruits. I will say that more often than not, I use canned fruits.

2 cups peach halves

2 1/2 cups pineapple chunks

2 cups pear halves

1 small bottle maraschino cherries

2 1/2 cups sliced apples

1/3 cup butter

3/4 cup brown sugar

4 teaspoons curry powder

1. **Drain the fruit** overnight if using canned fruits in the refrigerator. You can drain all of the fruit together.

2. **Preheat your oven to 325 degrees.**

3. **Place your fruits** in a 1 1/2 quart casserole dish. I do remember this dish was typically served in a round or oval casserole dish and that is how I prepare the dish.

4. **Melt the butter and add the brown sugar and curry. Spoon over fruit.**

5. **Bake for 1 hour uncovered.** Allow to cool enough to **refrigerate this dish overnight**, covered. Before serving **reheat at 325 degrees** for 20 minutes. It does not have to be refrigerated and then reheated.

6. Serve warm with ham, lamb or poultry or brunch grits, bacon, etc.

a Southern Legacy

sausage gravy casserole

Dick and I really enjoy a great biscuit with a yummy sausage gravy. We seek places that claim to have the best biscuits and gravy. I enjoy sampling, especially when I can talk to the cook or chef to find out their personal secret to their wonderful gravy. You want a sausage gravy with a little peppery taste, not floury, that is super creamy and thick. I believe many people share this love. I wanted a way to give large groups of people all of those flavors without having to figure out a way to keep the gravy warm. This casserole hits all the marks.

1 pound breakfast sausage

1/2 small onion, diced

1 stick of butter

1/2 cup all-purpose flour

1 1/2 cups milk

1 teaspoon pepper

2 cups self-rising flour

1 stick butter, grated

1/2 cup buttermilk

6 eggs

1 cup cheese, shredded

1/2 cup milk

salt and pepper to taste

1. **Preheat your oven to 350 degrees. Grease a 9 x 13 casserole pan.**

2. **Brown the sausage and onions** in skillet. Onions are an important part of a good sausage gravy.

3. Now you are going to create a roux for this dish. **Add butter to coat the sausage and onions**. Once the butter has melted, **add the flour** and stir for about 2 minutes. It takes a bit of time for this mixture to cook to allow the flour taste to be cooked out.

4. **Add pepper and stir**. Switch to a whisk. **Slowly add in the milk** and let the gravy thicken. Now you could stop right here and place this mixture on toast or a biscuit, and be very happy. I encourage you to continue.

5. In a medium bowl, **combine self-rising flour, grated butter and buttermilk. Stir** until just combined. **Drop** this biscuit dough mixture by spoonfuls into the bottom of a well greased 9 x 13 casserole pan.

6. **Layer shredded cheese** over the biscuit mixture.

7. **Whisk together** the eggs and milk. **Add** the additional salt and pepper and **pour** over the casserole.

8. **Pour the sausage gravy over the entire mixture.**

9. **Bake for 35-45 minutes**, or until eggs and biscuits are cooked through.

10. **Serve warm** (leftovers are excellent too!).

a Southern Legacy

eggs sunday night style

I have great memories surrounding this recipe. Do you remember hash browns dried and in a box? That is how this recipe first began. My Mom made it for many Sunday night meals because we had Sunday supper after church. It is filling and a great way to have a little breakfast for dinner. After my senior prom I invited 8 - 10 other couples to come to my house for breakfast. Mom made several batches of this recipe. The hash browns are creamy, the Canadian bacon gets a crunch on the edges and then everyone gets their own egg.
I can't think about my senior prom without remembering this recipe.

1 bag fresh or frozen hash brown
    potatoes OR 4 Russet Potatoes,
    peeled and grated
2 tablespoons butter
1/4 cup flour
1/2 stick butter
1/2 teaspoon salt
1 cup milk
1 cup sour cream
10 - 12 slices Canadian Bacon
8 eggs
Chopped Parsley

1. **Preheat oven to 350 degrees.**
2. **If using frozen or bagged potatoes, heat a large cast iron or non-stick sauce pan on high. Melt 2 tablespoons butter. Add potatoes** in an even layer. Leave them alone. Let them brown on the first side. Flip in sections. Let them brown on the second side. **If using fresh potatoes, peel and grate, then squeeze the water out of them** and then start the frying process. You want caramelization on these potatoes.
3. Next **make a white sauce using flour, salt, butter, milk and sour cream. Melt the butter** in a sauce pan. **Add the flour** and whisk for 1— 2 minutes. Do not brown the butter and flour mixture. You are cooking to help remove the flour taste. **Add the milk and sour cream.** Whisk until the sauce thickens.
4. In a large bowl. **Stir together the hash browns, parsley and the white sauce.**
5. **Spoon** into a greased 9 x 13 casserole dish.
6. **Place** bacon, over-lapped, down center of the casserole. Bake for 15 minutes. Remove from oven. Make a well for each egg on either side of the Canadian bacon. Add eggs. Place back in the oven until eggs are set to desired doneness. Do not over cook the eggs. No one wants a rubbery egg.

a Southern Legacy

maple bacon grilled cheese

Isn't Pinterest the best web app? I love that you can search for so many things and then store them on your own boards. I found myself searching through Pinterest one day looking for something I could make for a food based fundraiser in our area for 400 guests. I saw a version of this on Pinterest. There are some important steps to follow so read through this all the way before beginning. The good news is that you can make 400 of them in about 2 hours with the help of some great sous chefs and two electric fry pans. Just imagine a grilled cheese with a hint of cinnamon and topped with bacon and maple syrup. Such a delicious combination! This recipe makes one serving.

2 pieces of bacon

2 tablespoons maple syrup

2 slices good white bread

1 egg, plus 1 egg yolk

1/2 teaspoon cinnamon

2 tablespoons milk

1 tablespoons butter

3 tablespoons grated cheddar cheese

3 tablespoons grated Monterey Jack cheese

1. **Fry the bacon** until crispy. **Rough chop the bacon** and place in a bowl. **Add syrup** and set aside.

2. Heat a cast iron pan and **melt 1 tablespoon butter** in the pan.

3. In a bowl, **add the egg, additional yolk, cinnamon and milk. Whisk** to combine. **Dip** only one side of each slice of bread in the egg mixture. **Grill** only the wet side of each slice of bread. Move to your work surface.

4. On one of the grilled sides **add the cheeses. Place** another grilled side down on top of the cheeses. Dip the sandwich in egg mixture and **grill** on both sides..

5. **Place** on serving plate and cut in half. **Pour** bacon maple mixture over and enjoy!

easy cinnamon rolls

My family loves cinnamon rolls. That means I need a way to make good, easy and quick cinnamon rolls on demand. I have created the answer! God bless puffed pastry and pizza dough. As long as I keep one or the other on hand I can make cinnamon rolls happen on the spur of the moment. Now let's talk about the glaze on the cinnamon rolls. I am not a glaze person on my cinnamon rolls. I just like butter. However, I do like playing with the glaze flavoring for others. I think the coffee creamer option is a lot of fun and offers tons of variety.

1/2 cup cinnamon

1/2 cup brown sugar

1 puffed pastry sheet, thawed but chilled or pre-made refrigerated pizza dough

1/2 stick butter, softened

raisins, optional

pecans or walnuts or your favorite nuts, optional

3/4 cup powdered sugar

1 - 3 tablespoons of milk

1 teaspoon brewed coffee, maple syrup, vanilla or almond extract (you can even use flavored coffee creamers)

1. **Preheat oven to 400 degrees.**
2. **Mix cinnamon and sugar** in a small bowl. It is important to mix these together. This keeps the cinnamon from tasting bitter on the cinnamon roll.
3. **Place puffed pastry** in the refrigerator the night before. You do not want it frozen and definitely not room temperature. Take one sheet and unfold the puffed pastry. **If using pizza dough,** let it rest on the counter for 15 minutes. Then stretch and roll it into a large rectangular shape. **Take the softened butter** and smear it all over one side of the pastry/dough. **Generously apply** cinnamon and sugar mixture. **Add** as many raisins and nuts as you would like.
4. **Start rolling** the puffed pastry/dough from the edge closest to you. Roll tight. Cut into 2" slices. **Generously butter** a cake pan. Place each roll in the pan and press it slightly into the pan. Leave a little room in between.
5. **Bake for 20 - 25 minutes**.
6. While the rolls are baking, **mix together** powdered sugar, milk and the flavoring of your choice. Whisk for 1 minute. This will be the glaze for the cinnamon rolls.
7. Let the cinnamon rolls cool slightly. Then **glaze as desired.**

mama's coffee cake

I believe coffee cakes need to make a big come back. They can provide breakfast for the whole week. A coffee cake is not necessarily super sweet and you can change flavors each week. Also, typically they are so easy to assemble! The texture makes you want to push your fork into the crumbs to gather every bite. I can picture my great-grandmother making her coffee cake and stopping mid-morning with a cup of coffee to enjoy a break. She was a very hardworking woman. I am positive that the crunch of the coffee cake and the moist texture was the perfect compliment to her morning coffee.

2 sticks butter, softened

1 cup sugar

2 eggs

1 teaspoon vanilla extract

2 cups all-purpose flour

1 teaspoon baking soda

1 teaspoon baking powder

1 cup sour cream

1 cup brown sugar

2 1/2 teaspoons cinnamon

1/2 cup pecans or walnuts, chopped

1. **Preheat oven to 350 degrees.**
2. In a stand mixer bowl, **cream butter and sugar.**
3. **Add the eggs** one at a time. Add extract.
4. **Add** baking soda, baking powder and flour. **Add** sour cream.
5. **Pour** half of the batter into a greased, square pan. Typically I use an 8 x 8 square pan.
6. In a small bowl, **combine** brown sugar, cinnamon and nuts. **Sprinkle half** the nut mixture on batter. **Pour rest** of batter on top and spread. **Sprinkle** rest of topping.
7. **Bake for 40 minutes. Cut into squares and enjoy.**

english muffin bread

I never, ever, thought about making my own English Muffins until the recipe was passed along to me. Once you have you will wonder why you have not made these all of your life. My mother-in-law, Charmane, sent this recipe to me when I married Dick. Dick and I love it. The bread is best right out of the oven (as all bread is, right?). I slice the leftover loaf and freeze the slices individually. Then we take one slice out at a time, place it in the toaster (frozen). All that remains is to top with some butter and some homemade apple butter. It makes the morning so much better.

---

5 cups all-purpose flour, divided

1 tablespoon sugar

2 teaspoons salt

1/4 teaspoon baking soda

2 packages rapid rise yeast

2 cups milk

1/2 cup water

cornmeal or semolina, for dusting

1. **Preheat oven to 400 degrees. Set aside one cup of flour.** You will need this extra flour later wfor stiffening up the batter.
2. In a large bowl, **combine** the 4 cups of the flour, sugar, salt, soda and yeast.
3. **Heat liquids** together until very warm (125° to 130°). **Add the warm liquids to the dry ingredients.** Combine throughly. The dough will not form a ball.
4. **Stir in** reserved flour as needed to make a stiff batter.
5. **Grease and sprinkle** cornmeal or semolina in 2 loaf pans. Spoon batter into pans. Allow to rise in a warm place for 30 minutes.
6. **Bake for 25 minutes.** Remove from pans to cool immediately.
7. Once cooled you can **slice into 1" pieces.** Place them between waxed paper or parchment paper, place in a freezer bag. Freeze these and take a slice out at a time to toast in your toaster oven.

college crepes

In college, even back in the 1980's, poor college students consumed ramen noodles. That was never appealing to me. I learned about crepes my junior year at Berry College. I lived in a trailer which meant I had a kitchen and was no longer a slave to the dining hall. I discovered crepes were as cheap as ramen noodles. I could fill them with simple things and have a meal. You can even use your left-over Chinese food as a filling. Simply serve them folded with butter or add something to the center. For a dessert add your favorite pie filling. For a savory crepe add chicken salad or creamed shrimp. The ingredients are cheap and the results are delicious.

2 whole eggs

2 egg yolks, keep the egg white and
    scramble as a filling, if desired

1 1/2 cups milk

1 1/2 cups all purpose four

1 tablespoon sugar

1/4 cup butter, melted

Additional melted butter for cooking

Fillings of choice

1. You can bring this batter together with a bowl and a whisk, in a blender or a food processor.

2. **Add all ingredients and whisk**, blend or process until smooth. Let the batter rest for 20 minutes.

3. If you have a crepe pan that is wonderful. Otherwise a nonstick pan in good condition works.

4. **Heat pan on medium heat. Brush with melted butter.** Using a measuring cup or ladle, **spoon enough batter** into the pan just to coat the bottom. You will want to swirl the pan while filling to evenly coat the bottom. This all sounds very chef-y right now. As you make more and more you will find it is super simple. Typically the first crepe is not your prettiest. You need to understand your heat and pan and then crepes come out lovely each time.

5. **Return pan to heat. Cook** until the crepe is not shiny on the side you can see. Use a non-metal spatula to flip. You don't want to scratch this pan.

6. **Cook for 30 seconds or less**. Slide onto a dinner plate. You can stack crepes on top of each other. They do not stick. When filling you can fold them into fourths, halves or roll. Each technique works.

a Southern Legacy

cottage cream pancakes

I think I have as many pancake recipes as I do pound cake recipes. I selected this recipe for this book because it is so easy to assemble and holds well in the refrigerator. I can make pancakes many mornings in a row with little to no effort. I like this version because the inside is actually creamy. By the way, I grew up eating homemade apple butter on my pancakes, not maple syrup. My family loves pancakes for breakfast and dinner.

3 eggs

1 cup cottage cheese

3/4 sour cream

1/2 teaspoon lemon juice

3/4 teaspoon salt

1/2 teaspoon baking soda

1 cup flour

Butter for cooking

1. In a food processor or blender, **add all ingredients.** Process or blend until smooth.
2. **Let the batter rest** for 10 - 15 minutes. This step is important. Be patient.
3. **Heat a cast iron skillet or griddle**. Once the pan is heated, reduce your heat to medium. **Add a pat of butter. Pour batter** into a 3 - 4 inch circle. When you see bubbles, **flip your pancake. Cook** for another 30 - 45 seconds.
4. **Serve warm** with salted butter, maple syrup, jelly or apple butter. It is a great way to start the day!

cranberry fruit nut bread

I just love cranberries. Fresh cranberries are not the cranberries of the jellied version found in a can. Fresh cranberries are crisp and tart and dried cranberries make a great snack. Maybe one day I will create a cookbook with only cranberry recipes. This recipe became part of my life in my early 20's. At the time I only made it during November and December. I could not get fresh cranberries any other time. Now I buy many bags of cranberries in November and freeze them for cranberry yumminess all year long!

2 cups all-purpose flour

1 teaspoon salt

1 teaspoon orange zest

1 cup sugar

1/2 teaspoon baking soda

1 1/2 teaspoons baking powder

3/4 cup orange juice

1/4 cup Crisco or butter

1 egg, beaten

1 cup whole cranberries, coarsely chopped

1/2 cup chopped pecans or walnuts

Butter for greasing your pans

1. **Preheat oven to 350 degrees**.
2. In a medium bowl, **whisk all dry ingredients** together. **Add** orange zest and coat with flour.
3. Using a fork, **cut in shortening or butter.** Basically, you want to break the shortening up into small pieces that get coated with flour. You are looking for pea sized pieces.
4. In a small bowl **combine orange juice and egg. Add** to the dry ingredients. **Mix** until just combined.
5. **Fold in** cranberries and nuts.
6. **Put batter** in a greased loaf pan. I prefer to grease my loaf pan with butter. Make sure to get the sides and corners.
7. **Bake for one hour**. Cool in the pan for 10 minutes. Run a knife around the edges and remove loaf. Let it cool for the best results.

bacon gravy

Over the last five years, I have become a culinary instructor. I have found that teaching is something I truly enjoy. During my time at The Cook's Warehouse, a local kitchen store with an amazing teaching kitchen, I have become known as the Bacon Chef. Quarterly, I try to offer an "all bacon" class. We have made bacon baklava, bacon marshmallows and many, many other bacon inspired dishes. Bacon is certainly one of my personal basic food groups. I love sausage gravy and decided there must be a way to make bacon into an equally delicious gravy. After several experiments this recipe developed. I love both kinds of gravy and now I can make either based on which protein I have in my house.

6 slices thick bacon, cooked,
    save bacon fat

1 shallot, minced

1/4 cup bacon drippings

1/4 cup all-purpose flour

1 teaspoon salt or to taste

**1 teaspoon ground black pepper
or to taste**

1/2 teaspoon garlic powder

4 cups milk, divided

1. **Cook bacon** until crispy. It is important to have crispy bacon for this gravy. To cook bacon to a perfect crispy texture, place it in a hot pan. Do not over crowd the pan with bacon. Give the bacon its space. Do not move the bacon until you start to see brown on the edges. Flip the bacon and allow it to cook about half the time it cooked on the first side. Flip the bacon one more time and allow to cook for 30 - 45 seconds. Remove bacon to paper towels to drain.

2. **Leave about 1/4 cup of the bacon fat remaining.** If you don't have 1/4 of a cup add butter to make up the difference.

3. Add the minced shallot and cook for 2 minutes. I do like using a shallot for this recipe but you could substitute an onion.

4. **Whisk flour** into drippings and shallot until smooth. **Reduce heat** to low and cook the flour mixture until it turns a caramel brown color, stirring constantly, about 10 - 15 minutes. Be careful, the roux burns easily.

5. **Stir in** garlic powder, salt and black pepper.

6. **Whisk 1/2 cup milk** into the roux until thoroughly blended. Continue whisking milk into the gravy, 1/2 cup at a time, whisking in each amount of milk completely before adding more.

7. **Chop bacon. Add to gravy.** Bring gravy to a simmer and whisk constantly until thick, smooth, and bubbling.

8. **Serve** over a Southern biscuit, hash brown or a piece of toast.

mama's banana bread

MaMa was my Grandmother Hodges' mom (my great grandmother on my dad's side of the family). She was an excellent baker. I can remember standing in her kitchen watching her bake as I waited to go fishing with Papa. She also believed the only type of flour to use is White Lily and I have to agree. White Lily is light and low in protein. It makes a big difference when you are baking a cake or making biscuits. If you can not get White Lily Flour, try King Arthur, a good second choice. A good banana bread recipe is handy because you now have breakfast, a snack or for a banana bread and cream cheese sandwich. Try using a slice the next day for French Toast. You can also make muffins using this recipe.

2 sticks butter

1 cup brown sugar

2 eggs

3 bananas, mashed with a fork

1 cup chopped nuts (pecans or walnuts are my choices)

2 cups (plain) White Lily Flour - plain flour is all-purpose

1 teaspoon baking soda

1/2 teaspoon salt

1. **Preheat oven to 350 degrees.**
2. Using a stand mixer or a hand mixer. **Cream butter and sugar** until fluffy. This takes about 3 minutes.
3. **Add eggs** one at a time. Beat well.
4. **Add** mashed bananas and nuts. **Stir** to combine.
5. In a bowl, **combine** flour, salt and baking soda. **Whisk.** This helps to add air to the flour. **Add** whisked flour mixture slowly to the wet batter.
6. **Bake** in a greased loaf pan or small muffin tins. For loaf pan bake for one hour. For muffins, bake for 20 - 25 minutes.

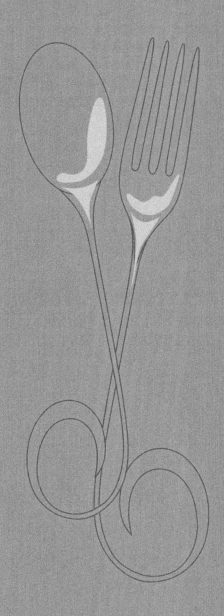

lunching around

lime salad

A fun, light green, marshmallow dotted side dish is a childhood dream. Jello is a big part of my childhood and young adult life. Sunday dinners and holiday gatherings always included a Jello dish. It was a guarantee that if you, as a child, couldn't find anything to eat, the Jello dish would always make it better. When I grew up it was one of the first dishes my mother would give you as the "dish" for you to bring to a gathering. If you mastered Jello you might be given a vegetable side dish the next time!
Bring back the Jello dishes!

2 cups boiling water

1 package lime Jello, large

8 ounces cream cheese

1/4 cup mayonnaise

1 tablespoon milk

1 can crushed pineapple, drained

1/2 cup chopped pecans

1 bag small marshmallows

1. **Mix together the boiling water and lime Jello.** Cover and place in the refrigerator until the Jello just starts to set
2. In a large bowl **beat together the cream cheese, mayonaisse and milk. Whisk in Jello.**
3. **Stir in pineapple, nuts and marshmallows.**
4. **Put in** Jello mold or casserole dish. **Cover and refrigerate.**

tomato aspic

Tomato aspic is a dish that my Mom and Aunt Sue absolutely love.
It has never gone out of style at our house. Tomato Aspic usually makes an
appearance at Easter and occasionally at picnics or pot luck events.
My Mom prefers celery and olives in hers. You can add artichoke hearts,
additional chopped onions and hearts of palm. Aspics became a society
lunch or dinner staple in the 1950's. They are, at their base,
a salad with an impressive presentation.

4 cups tomato juice

1/3 onion, chopped

1/4 cup celery leaves, chopped

2 tablespoons brown sugar

1 teaspoon salt

2 small bay leaves

4 whole cloves

---

3 envelopes unflavored gelatin

3/4 cup cold water

3 tablespoons lemon juice

1 cup green olives, drained and diced

1 cup celery, diced

1. In a sauce pan, **combine tomato juice, onion, celery leaves, brown sugar, salt, bay leaves and cloves. Simmer** over medium low heat for 5 minutes.

2. While the mixture is simmering, **soften gelatin in the cold water**.

3. **Strain tomato mixture** into a medium bowl. **Add softened gelatin** and stir until dissolved.

4. **Add lemon juice.**

5. **Pour this mixture** into a 5 - 6 cup serving dish or into individuals ramekins.

6. **Allow to partially set. Add olives and celery.**

7. **Chill** until set.

8. **Serve** with a dollop of homemade mayonnaise or a slice of avocado.

tart asparagus salad

I considered Mrs. Peggy Dosser Benson to be a part of my family.
She was my grandmother's good friend and a tremendous role model to me.
She worked very hard to promote the Arts in Cobb County. It is because of her
and one other person that I worked in the arts for 29 years in Cobb County.
I couldn't begin to thank her enough for her role in my life. I had many fundraising
and planning meeting luncheons in her home. This dish was often served.
Some may call this an aspic. As a Southerner I know the value of a great aspic.
Try it. You will be surprised by how much you enjoy it.

2 envelopes unflavored gelatin

1/2 cup cold water

1 teaspoon salt

pot of water

1/3 cup sugar

1/2 cup white vinegar

1 cup asparagus water

   (save water from the blanching process)

1 tablespoon onion, minced

2 tablespoons lemon juice

1 bunch asparagus

1 cup roasted red pepper, cut into strips

1 teaspoon salt

5 ounce can water chestnuts, sliced

1 cup celery, chopped

1. **Dissolve gelatin** in the cold water.
2. **To blanch the asparagus: bring a pot of water to a boil. Add 1 tablespoon of salt. Add asparagus** for 3 minutes. **Place asparagus** in a bowl of ice water to stop cooking process. **Save one cup** of the blanching water. This is asparagus water! **Cut asparagus** into 2" pieces.
3. **Combine sugar, vinegar, and 1 cup asparagus water. Bring to a boil. Remove** from heat; **add** gelatin, onion, and lemon juice. Allow to cool, then **add** asparagus, red pepper, 1 teaspoon salt, water chestnuts, and celery.
4. **Pour** into a 1 1/2 quart mold or Bundt cake pan and chill until set.
5. To assist in the unmolding process, **fill a large bowl with hot water. Dip the outer edges of the mold** used in the hot water. This will slightly melt the gelatin allowing the salad to slip out onto a serving platter.

a Southern Legacy

homemade mayonnaise

Every Southern girl should know how to make homemade mayonnaise. It is a treat. You can make a great egg or chicken salad with homemade mayonnaise. It is a wonderful garnish on the tart asparagus salad and tomato aspic. I would serve it on a hamburger as well. The process is not difficult. Any blender makes this recipe easy and non-threatening.

1 egg

1 teaspoon apple cider vinegar

1 teaspoon salt

Pinch of ground pepper

1/2 teaspoon sugar

1 1/2 cups oil (not extra virgin)

Juice of 1 lemon

1. In a food processor or blender, **add egg, vinegar, salt, pepper and sugar.** Pulse 4 - 6 times.
2. Next you are going to **stream in the oil**. This steaming technique is important so that your mayonnaise emulsifies or comes together. **Turn on your machine and slowly add the oil.**
3. Once the oil is added, **finish with the juice of one lemon**. Refrigerate.
4. This mayonnaise is best when made a day before you want to serve it.

mrs. ann's chinese coleslaw

Mrs. Ann is a great cook, mother of my childhood best friend and a member of my Mom's bridge club. She always had wonderful treats at her house and I can remember Mom talking about the food at her parties. I know her Christmas cookie tray is one of my favorite treats. I treasure any recipe shared by her. I believe I have been making this dish for several decades. It is perfect for a pot-luck and great with BBQ. Because of the ramen noodles, this recipe doesn't keep well over night; however leftovers are not usually an issue because it is so good!

Coleslaw

1/2 head Savoy cabbage, sliced thin

4 green onions, chopped

2 tablespoons sliced or slivered almonds, toasted

8 tablespoons sesame seeds, toasted

1 package ramen noodles, crushed,
        flavor packet discarded

1. In a large bowl, **layer the Coleslaw ingredients.**

2. **In a large mason jar add all of the dressing ingredients.** Microwave for 1 minute to dissolve sugar. Add the lid and **shake vigorously**. Set aside until just before serving.

3. **Toss the salad** with dressing 10 minutes before serving.

Dressing

4 tablespoons sugar

1 teaspoon salt

1 teaspoon pepper

3/4 cup canola or vegetable oil

6 tablespoons rice vinegar

mom's reunion salad

My Mom really enjoys this salad. Every good Southern girl knows how important it is to have a good pot luck green salad in her recipe box. It is best prepared the day ahead, however, I have never turned it down when just made! I like to hold the bacon out and top with the bacon just before service. I like my bacon crispy, not soggy.

1 large head broccoli

1 small red onion

1/2 cup raisins

1/2 cup pecans, chopped

3/4 cup mayonaisse

2 tablespoons milk

2 tablespoons white vinegar

1/3 cup Splenda or sweetener of your choice

   (you can exchange these two in equal amounts)

salt and pepper to taste

4 slices bacon, cooked and crumbled

1. **Clean, trim and chop broccoli** into a large bowl. **Cut the top and bottom off** the red onion. **Cut the onion** in half so that you can slice it into "half-moon" shaped slices.

2. **Add** onion, raisins and pecans to the large bowl.

3. In a small bowl, **whisk together mayonaisse, milk, vinegar and sweetener.** Whisk until smooth. **Pour dressing** over salad. **Add salt and pepper** to taste.

4. **Cover and refrigerate** overnight.

5. **Top with bacon** crumbles before serving.

spinach & artichoke stuffed tomatoes

Simply put, the tomato in this recipe allows you to eat spinach and artichoke
dip as a side dish. Life is good when you find a good vehicle for artichokes!
I serve this for luncheons, as an appetizer and during the summer
when tomatoes are perfect.

---

4 to 5 Roma tomatoes or small tomatoes

**10 ounce package frozen chopped
spinach, thawed and drained**

14.5 ounce can artichokes, drained well

4 ounce package cream cheese

1/3 cup mayonnaise

1/4 cup Parmesan cheese, grated

1/2 teaspoon salt

Hot sauce

1. **Slice Roma tomatoes** in half lengthwise and gut out the middle. Place on paper towels to drain.
2. In a mixer fitted with a metal whip or food processor fitted with the plastic blade, **combine** spinach, artichokes, cream cheese, mayonnaise, Parmesan, salt and hot sauce to taste and mix or process well.
3. **Add 1 drop** of hot sauce at a time to taste. That's right, taste your food to know if it is seasoned well. You can look at it all day, but until you taste it you will never know.
4. **Fill Roma tomatoes** with spinach mixture and place on a baking sheet.
5. Tomatoes can be covered and refrigerated at this point for up to 2 days.
6. **Bake at 350 degrees** for 15 to 20 minutes.
7. Filling should just be heated through. Overcooking will make a tomato mess.
8. **Serve** warm or at room temperature. Substituting another can of artichokes for the spinach also makes a wonderful stuffing.

fruited rice

Here is the story behind my love of this fruited rice dish. It is a great dish for luncheons, but that is not why there's a story with this recipe. I worked for the Cobb County Parks Department, in the Cultural Affairs Division, for 29 years. As you can guess, I worked with many men. They were certainly meat and potatoes types of guys. That fact did not stop me from preparing this dish for a lunch meeting one day. Years later they tease me about putting fruit in rice. They simply couldn't understand the pairing. I have since found many men who enjoy the pairing; however, I will always smile when any male takes a bite of this dish.

3 tablespoons butter

1/4 cup green onion, peeled and chopped

1/2 cup celery, chopped

1 cup white uncooked long grain rice

14.5 ounce can chicken broth

3/4 cup milk

1/2 teaspoon salt

1/8 teaspoon pepper

1/3 cup chopped almonds (or other favorite nut)

1/8 cup dried cranberries

1/4 cup dried apricots, diced

1/2 cup purple grapes, halved

1/4 teaspoon cinnamon

1. **Melt butter** in a medium skillet and **cook onion and celery** for 2 to 3 minutes. **Add rice** and cook for 2 minutes while stirring constantly.

2. **Add broth, milk, salt and pepper. Cook** covered for 10 to 15 minutes. **Remove from heat,** and when rice is just tender, remove half of the rice and rinse under cold water. This will give the rice a fluffy texture.

3. **Add dried fruits** to hot rice and **stir** well.

4. **Add the remaining rice** and store in a bowl or storage bag until ready to serve, up to 2 days.

5. **Reheat rice** in microwave with one ice cube. The ice cube helps to steam the rice.

6. **Toss with grapes and cinnamon** and serve in a crystal or china serving bowl with a bunch of purple grape garnishes.

A special thank you to Kathleen Rambo Howard for sharing this recipe with me.

chicken salad with avacados

In the South, there are as many chicken salad recipes as there are people with opinions about which one is the best. My Mom has played bridge with the same group of southern women for 53 years. When they began playing bridge together the house had to be perfect, the hostess prepared a lovely "ladies who lunch" type meal and the good china made an appearance. Today, they just bring a chocolate dessert. One member of this group, Mrs. Anne, taught me how wonderful tarragon is in chicken salad. I have a hard time making any version of it without tarragon.
My version of tarragon chicken salad uses no mayonnaise.
Creating a chicken salad without mayonnaise is considered unusual,
but a great idea when serving at a picnic or an outdoor concert.

1 rotisserie chicken

    (makes life so much easier)

1/3 cup olive oil, not extra virgin

1/2 teaspoon salt

1/2 teaspoon pepper

1 teaspoon dried tarragon or

    2 teaspoons fresh, chopped

Juice and zest of one lemon

1 Granny Smith apple, diced

1 avocado, diced

Variations : Substitute 2 diced peaches for the apple and a lime for the lemon.

1. **Pick all of the meat** from the rotisserie chicken and place in a medium sized bowl. This is easiest to do when the chicken is still warm. Shred the meat with a fork. You can also put the meat in a food processor and pulse 4 - 6 times if you like the chicken meat very fine in your chicken salad.

2. In a bowl, **whisk together the olive oil, lemon, tarragon, salt and pepper.**

3. **Add chopped apple and avocado** to the chicken. **Pour** the dressing over the mixture. **Stir** to combine. **Serve!**

a Southern Legacy

frozen cherry salad

This recipe is for my sister Lea. To her, this is perfect with chicken salad and cheese straws. We learned to eat these things together by having lunch at the Swan Coach House in Atlanta. We both order this combination every time we go there. This recipe is cold and perfect for a summer gathering. For years it has been served all over the South in tea rooms and private homes. There is something magical about a little pink frozen fruit dish.

8 ounce package cream cheese,
    room temperature
8 ounce container Cool Whip, thawed
21 ounce can cherry pie filling
2 (11 ounce) cans mandarin oranges, drained
1 cup maraschino cherries, chopped
1 cup pecans, chopped (optional)

1. In a large bowl, **combine cream cheese and Cool Whip** until smooth. You can do that with a hand mixer.
2. **Fold in the pie filling, oranges, cherries and nuts** (if desired) with a large spoon or spatula.
3. **Place in ramekin** cups and then on a baking sheet that fits in your freezer. Cover and freeze until serving.
4. I like to remove them from the ramekins to serve. **Dip the ramekin in hot water** for 10 seconds and the salad should come out easily.

curry deviled eggs

Deviled eggs are one of the best parts of my life. I could certainly add my family's olive deviled egg recipe or the pickle relish version to my first cookbook, but I chose this recipe because it is unique. I came up with this version as an appetizer for a party. In my adult life I have become a fan of curry. This deviled egg is different, savory and delicious. You may have skeptics when they hear the name of the egg, you will have fans once they taste it!

12 eggs

3 tablespoons Hellman's Mayonnaise

2 teaspoons curry powder

1/2 teaspoon salt

1/4 cup unsweetened shredded coconut

1/4 cup golden raisins

1 teaspoon cilantro, minced

1. **Place eggs** in a large pot. **Cover with water** about 1" above the top of the eggs. **Bring to a boil**. **Turn off eggs** and let them sit in the hot water for 10 minutes. **Drain. Cover** with ice. Let them sit for at least 30 minutes. **Peel** the eggs.

2. **Cut the eggs** in half. **Place yolks** in a medium bowl. **Place egg whites** on your egg tray.

3. **Add the mayonaisse, curry and salt to the egg yolks. Mash and stir** with a large fork until well combined.

4. **Add coconut, raisins and cilantro.**

5. Take the **yolk mixture and add it to a large plastic baggie**. Cut a 3/4" piece off one corner of the baggie. **Pipe the mixture** into your egg whites. **Chill and serve.**

bacon marmalade

I am dedicating this recipe to our nephew, Jude McNamara. I created this dish while in Houston, Texas for my mother-in-law's 80th birthday. The entire family gathered in Texas and I cooked for them all. I had the idea for this recipe for months. The night I made this final version, I reached for dark rum as an addition. Why dark rum? My husband loves a good Dark and Stormy beverage. The dark rum was nearby so I decided to add it. Jude was my official taste tester that night. He ate so much food (including this recipe) that we found him later groaning and in a "food coma". Perfection!!

---

1 pound thick cut smoked bacon

1 medium yellow onion, chopped

3 cloves garlic, minced

1/2 cup dark rum

8 dates, chopped,

    or 3/4 cup chopped dates

6 tablespoons brown sugar

1/2 cup apple cider vinegar

1/2 cup maple syrup

    (regular pancake syrup will work in a pinch)

2 cups freshly brewed coffee

    (I have used instant coffee)

6 dashes Tabasco chipotle pepper sauce

6 grinds of fresh black pepper

I serve this with pimento cheese or over grilled meats, and I have even used it as a mix-in for brownies.

1. In a cast iron skillet, **cook the bacon** until crisp. **Save** 3 tablespoons of bacon fat. Set bacon aside. When cooled, crumble the bacon.

2. In the cast iron pan with the 3 tablespoons of bacon fat, **add onions and garlic. Cook** until the onions are caramelized. Stir often so that the garlic doesn't burn or over brown.

3. **Add** chopped dates,.and the brown sugar. **Cook** mixture for 3 minutes.

4. You will **add the liquids one at a time.** Give them time to become one with everything else to make the perfect marmalade. Don't dump everything in at once. Layering flavor is the only way to go! **Add dark rum** and cook for 3 – 5 minutes on medium heat. **Add the vinegar** and cook for 3 – 5 minutes. **Add the syrup** and cook for another 3- 5 minutes.

5. **Add** the coffee and return crumbled bacon to the pan. **Stir** and turn the heat to medium low. Now let this simmer until the liquid is almost gone. This takes about 30 – 45 minutes, so be patient.

6. At the very end, just before serving, **add** the Tabasco and pepper.

7. Sometimes I take half of the mixture and puree it with an immersion blender. Then I add it back. Sometimes I serve it as is. It really is great either way.

pimento cheese

This recipe has been a part of my family forever. I know forever seems like a really long time but it is true. I believe the addition of the grated red onion is what sets this recipe apart from many others. It is important to grate your own cheese and not to purchase grated cheese in a bag. The cheese in a bag has a floury coating to keep it from sticking together. You just don't need that floury stuff in your pimento cheese. I remember pimento cheese sandwiches on family trips, tailgating, weddings and at concerts. It is good on bread, in your mac-n-cheese, in a meatloaf, smeared on a hamburger or baked on a half of a jalapeño pepper.

16 ounces block of extra sharp cheddar cheese

1/2 cup Hellman's Mayonnaise (this brand is important)

4 ounce jar of diced pimentos, drained

1/4 of a medium red onion

1. In a large bowl, **grate the cheddar cheese**.
2. **Add the mayonaisse and drained pimentos**.
3. **Grate the red onion** into the mixture.
   I use a microplane for this task.
4. **Stir** until combined.

nibbles

When you are entertaining in the South, little Nibbles scattered throughout the party location or certainly at the bar area are important and should be very flavorful. Nuts are a good choice but why not mix it up with these Nibbles? My Grandmother Hodges left this recipe for me. My husband believes any nibble involving an oyster cracker must be worth eating! Nibbles are a wonderful added touch when entertaining. I can also recommend them in tomato soup.

16 ounces of oyster crackers

1 teaspoon garlic salt

1 teaspoon dried dill weed

1/2 teaspoon lemon pepper

1/2 cup vegetable oil

1 package ranch dressing mix

1. **Preheat oven to 350 degrees.**
2. In a medium bowl, **whisk together** everything except the crackers.
3. **Add** the crackers and gently toss to coat.
4. Place on a baking sheet. **Bake the crackers for 12 - 15 minutes.**
5. **Cool and store** in an air tight container.

peanut butter cookies

I made these so many times in 8th grade during home economics. At one point in time I had the recipe memorized. I was even called out of class on occasion to make them for visiting teachers and administrators. I didn't use a mixer at the time. Let me just say that using a mixer gets cookies in the oven faster.

1 cup Crisco

1 cup peanut butter, smooth or crunchy

1/2 teaspoon salt

1 cup sugar

1 cup light brown sugar

2 eggs, beaten

1 tablespoon milk

1/2 teaspoon baking soda

2 cups all-purpose flour

1. **Preheat oven to 325 degrees.**
2. In the bowl of your mixer, **combine Crisco, salt and peanut butter.**
3. **Add white and brown sugars**. Beat for 4 minutes.
4. **Add eggs** one at a time.
5. **Add flour and baking soda.**
6. **Roll into a 1" ball.** Place on a baking sheet lined with parchment paper. **Flatten with a fork.**
7. **Bake for 15 - 20 minutes**. I like mine a little soft in the center so I like 15 minutes. Store in an airtight container.

a Southern Legacy

raspberry thumbprints

If I could only have one cookie the rest of my life, I believe I would select this one. It is a Christmas standard on my cookie trays. It is buttery, sweet and the glaze is what makes them absolutely perfect! They go right next to the peanut butter balls. I also like that they add a bit of color on the tray with the jelly. Feel free to change the jelly flavor.

The cookie

1 cup butter, softened

2/3 cup sugar

1/2 teaspoon almond extract

2 cups all-purpose flour

1/2 cup raspberry jam

The glaze

1 cup powdered sugar

1 1/2 teaspoons almond extract

2 to 3 teaspoons water

1. **Preheat oven to 350 degrees.**
2. In the bowl of a stand mixer, **cream butter, sugar and extract** until creamy, about 4 minutes.
3. **Add flour slowly** and beat until combined. **Cover. Refrigerate** for one hour.
4. **Shape dough into 1 inch balls.** Place balls 2 inches apart on ungreased cookie sheet.
5. Use measuring spoon or your thumb to **place an indentation** in each ball. **Add 1/4 teaspoon of jam to each cookie.**
6. **Bake 14 - 18 minutes.** Let stand 5 minute and then move to cooling rack.
7. **Mix glaze** ingredients and drizzle over cooled cookies.
8. **Store** in air tight container.

cherry wink cookies

Isn't it amazing how the sight and smell of a single item can flood your memory with thoughts of your childhood. I went decades without making and having these cookies. My first bite took me straight back to my childhood in the happiest of ways. My Mom learned to make these while my Dad was in college. She made them for my Grandmother Hodges as well and she fell in love with them. I remember having them often. They have a smooth center, a crunch outside and this great cherry in the center. They make me smile!

---

1 cup sugar

3/4 cup shortening

2 eggs

2 tablespoons milk

2 1/2 cups White Lily Flour, whisked

1 teaspoon baking powder

1/2 teaspoon salt

1/2 teaspoon baking soda

1 cup nuts, chopped

1 cup dates, chopped

1 cup corn flakes, crushed

Small jar maraschino cherries, whole

1. **Preheat oven to 375 degrees.**

2. In a mixer, **cream sugar and shortening** for 3 minutes. **Add eggs.** **Add** flour, baking powder, baking soda, salt, milk, nuts and dates.

3. If the dough seems soft, place the bowl in the refrigerator for about an hour.

4. **Shape into 1" balls.** I like to use a small ice cream scoop to help create the ball shape and to make sure each cookie is the same size. **Roll the ball** in crushed corn flakes. **Indent with thumb. Place a cherry** in each thumbprint.

5. **Bake for 12 - 14 minutes until golden.**

6. **Store** in an airtight container.

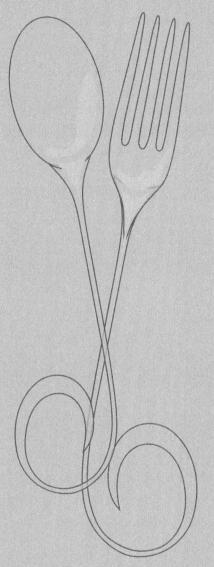

completely southern

black bing cherry salad

This Jello dish typically made an appearance at Hodges gatherings. I think the addition of 2 cups of Sherry makes this a more elegant tasting Jello dish. I am a big cherry fan and I really like Jello for a family meal.

1 tablespoon plain gelatin

1 1/4 cups cold water

2 small boxes of cherry Jello

2 cups cherry juice

   (this is juice left over from draining

   cherries, add water to get to 2 cups)

1 large can black bing cherries, pitted

1 cup pecans or walnuts, chopped

2 cups sweet sherry

1. **Dissolve gelatin** in 1/4 cup of cold water.
2. **Drain the can of cherries**. Save the juice. **Add** enough water to the juice to create 2 cups of liquid.
3. In a sauce pan **bring juice to a boil. Add** Jello and gelatin and stir to dissolve.
4. **Add** sherry, nuts and cherries.
5. **Place** in decorative mold or flat dish. **Chill until set.**

cranberry crunch

Cranberry Sauce is a Thanksgiving staple. This version is super crunchy and tart. The perfect Thanksgiving bite always includes cranberries in some form. I like to keep this around for turkey sandwiches. On wonderful bread, add sliced turkey, cranberry crunch, gravy and dressing. Now that is a leftover sandwich!

2 cups whole cranberries

1 cup sugar

Juice of one orange

1 small jar orange marmalade

2 oranges, zested

1/2 cup crystalized ginger

1 cup chopped nuts

1. **Preheat oven to 350 degrees**
2. In an 8 x 8 casserole dish, **add cranberries, sugar and orange juice. Stir. Cover with foil. Bake for 20 minutes.**
3. **Add** remaining ingredients. **Stir** to combine. **Store** in refrigerator.
4. If doubling the recipe, then double the cooking time.

This makes a great gift! You can place the mixture in a Mason Jar, tie a ribbon around the lid, and attach the recipe with ways to use this lovely cranberry dish.

vidalia onion dip

Vidalia onions are grown in Georgia. Do you want to know how to store these onions? Here is my Mom's method. You will need old panty hose, Vidalia onions, a porch and thumbtacks. You put the onion in the hose and tie a knot in-between each onion. Then tack the line of onions to the ceiling on your porch. As you need one you cut below a knot. Well that's how it happened at my house. Some recipes are simple. Sometimes simple is all you need. This recipe is easily decreased or increased. Simply keep all measurements the same as you go up or down.

2 cups Vidalia onions, chopped

2 cups Swiss cheese, grated fresh

2 cups Hellman's mayonnaise

   (my mayonnaise of choice)

Crackers and/or vegetable for serving

1. **Preheat oven to 325 degrees.**
2. **Combine all** ingredients in a medium bowl.
3. **Put mixture** in an 8 x 8 casserole pan.
4. **Bake for 25 minutes. Serve** with crackers or cut up vegetables.

Variation: Add 1 teaspoon fresh chopped thyme, tarragon or rosemary and add 3 cloves grated garlic.

layered pretzel strawberry salad

I think this should be a dessert, but it is technically a salad. Every child will love seeing this at a family gathering. Crunchy, sweet, creamy, Jello goodness. I have cut back on the sugar, added more strawberries and lightened the cream cheese layer. It is still delicious and I truly can't tell the difference. It holds up very well and my girlfriends will tell you it makes an excellent dish at the beach!

1 1/2 sticks of butter, melted

3/4 cup brown sugar, divided

2 1/2 cups crushed pretzels

6 ounce package strawberry Jello

2 cups boiling water

3 cups strawberries, sliced and chilled

8 ounce package light cream cheese

12 ounces light Cool Whip

1. **To make the crust, combine** butter, 3 tablespoons brown sugar and pretzels. Press into 13 x 9 baking dish. **Bake at 350°** for 10 minutes. Cool and set aside.

2. **Dissolve Jello** in boiling water. **Cool** slightly. **Stir in** strawberries. **Chill** until it begins to set.

3. **Blend** cream cheese and remaining brown sugar. **Fold in** Cool Whip. **Spread** on crust. **Pour** Jello mixture over cream cheese mixture. **Chill until set.**

elizabeth's easiest bbq pork ever!

I stumbled across coffee as a tenderizer almost 10 years ago. The greatest part is that you don't taste the coffee but the coffee breaks down the meat perfectly. If you are a pressure cooker person, this recipe is great for that cooking method as well. Refer to you manual to adjust the cooking time.

3 pounds pork loin (leanest)
    or pork shoulder (more fat)
    or butt (good fat)
1 1/2 cups brewed coffee
1/2 cup favorite BBQ sauce
1 onion, sliced

1. **Place onions**, sliced and broken apart, on the bottom of your slow cooker.
2. **Add pork.**
3. **Mix coffee and BBQ** sauce together. **Pour** over the pork.
4. **Set slow cooker** on low for 8 – 10 hours.
5. Use two forks to **pull apart the pork** while still hot or warm and still in the juice.
6. **Serve** on tacos, rolls or simply on a plate.

bacon blanket turkey

I can remember my Mom getting up very early on Thanksgiving morning to put the turkey in the oven. She would then baste the turkey every 15 minutes for hours. I truly appreciate her dedication to her bird. I, on the other hand, would prefer to create a self basting method for my turkey. Bacon is the perfect self basting method in my book! The bacon blanket keeps the turkey moist, adds great flavor and is a wonderful treat when the turkey comes out of the oven and is cooling.

1 Turkey

12 slices thick bacon

1 onion

1 lemon

4 garlic cloves

3 fresh sage sprigs

6 - 8 fresh thyme sprigs

salt

black pepper

1. **Make sure your turkey is completely thawed**. You can safely do this in your refrigerator for about 3 days.

2. **Remove the turkey** from its packaging. **Remove the giblets** from the cavity of the turkey. Save them for the gravy. **Rinse the turkey and pat it dry** with paper towels.

3. **Preheat the oven to 400 degrees.**

4. **Place the turkey in a roasting pan** with a rack for the turkey.

5. **Cut the onion and lemon** into fourths. **Stuff them into the cavity** of the turkey. **Add** the garlic, sage and thyme to the cavity as well. **Tie the turkey legs** together with cotton twine.

6. **Generously salt and pepper** the skin on the turkey

7. **To create the bacon blanket, place 6 slices of bacon** side by side on a cutting board. **Fold back pieces 1, 3 and 5. Lay a piece of bacon across** the flat pieces on your board. **Place pieces 1, 3, and 5 back in place. Lift slice 2,4 and 6. Lay another side of bacon across**. You are creating a basket weave pattern.

8. Once the bacon blanket is created, **carefully lift the blanket and place it on top of the seasoned turkey.**

9. **Bake the turkey for 15 minutes per pound. Place the turkey in the 400 degree oven for 20 minutes.** Turn the heat down to 350 degrees for the remaining cook time.

10. **The internal temperature of the turkey should reach 160 degrees**. To check the temperature put the thermometer in the breast and then in the thigh to check places for doneness.

a Southern Legacy

giblet gravy

My Mom always creates a turkey gravy with the giblets. What are those? The turkey pieces that come in the bag with the turkey that most people throw away. This recipe dates back to 1960. She wrote this recipe down in her homemade cookbook that she kept her most important and well used recipes. My stepfather, Watson, preferred giblet gravy. However, I preferred a giblet free gravy (you can leave the giblets out). Mom always made both! She must love us a lot!

Turkey liver, heart, gizzard as available, cooked

Turkey pan drippings

1/3 cup all-purpose flour

2 cups chicken or turkey stock or broth

Salt and pepper to taste

2 eggs, boiled

1. You can prepare this in the roasting pan you used to cook your turkey or transfer the drippings into a large sauce pan. **Heat the drippings over medium heat.**
2. **Whisk in the flour**. Let the flour cook for 2 minutes with the drippings.
3. **Add the broth and continue to whisk.** The mixture should thicken. **Add salt and pepper.**
4. **Chop the liver, gizzard and heart. Add to the gravy**. Turn the heat to low. Allow to **cook for 15 minutes**.
5. **Add the chopped cooked eggs** and serve in a gravy boat.

baked ham

This ham recipe reminds me and my husband of Easter. We have very specific memories of our Moms creating this spectacular ham. It looks so lovely with the pineapple and cloves. The glaze gives it a sweet crunch. You can bet that some great ham sandwiches follow the next day after this ham is served, if there is any leftover!

1 uncooked bone-in ham

   (Mom prefers Smithfield hams)

1 large can pineapple chunks, save juice

Whole Cloves

3/4 cup brown sugar

1. In a large roasting pan, **place the ham**, pretty side up. **Cook at 325 degrees** for 20 minutes per pound.

2. **Remove the ham** 30 minutes before the overall cooking time is completed.

3. **Score** the top of the ham in a diamond pattern.

4. **Secure a pineapple chunk** on each diamond with a clove.

5. **Mix together** the pineapple juice and brown sugar. Pour over the ham to form a glaze.

6. **Return the ham** to the oven for 30 final minutes. You can baste the ham every 10 minutes.

7. **Remove from the oven** and let it cool for at least 15 - 20 minutes. **Slice and serve.**

potato salad

It's a good day at the Weaver house when there is potato salad. My husband with his German background loves a good potato salad. Add that to a Southern family who loves this with BBQ, ham or even a hamburger and it is certainly a staple. This version has a unique ending step. Cooking the whisked eggs, vinegar and mustard changes the potato salad from a really good dish to an excellent dish. I hope your family enjoys your new potato salad version.

2 1/2 - 3 pounds of Yukon gold potatoes, cooked and cubed

10 eggs, hard boiled and chopped

2 stalks of celery, diced

1 onion, diced

salt and pepper to taste

1 cup mayonnaise

4 uncooked eggs, beaten

3/4 cup vinegar

1 tablespoon yellow mustard

3/4 cup sugar

1. In a large bowl **add** the cooled, cooked potatoes, chopped eggs, diced celery and diced onion.
2. **Add salt and pepper** to taste. I am always asked how much. Start with a good pinch and add more later IF you feel the dish needs more. **Add** the mayonaisse to the dish. Stir in gently.
3. In a medium sauce pan **add** uncooked eggs, vinegar and mustard. Whisk these ingredients together over medium low heat until it begins to thicken. **Remove** from the heat and **add** sugar. Then gently **fold** the heated mixture into the potato mixture.
4. You can **serve this hot/warm**. It is also good cold and even better on the second day.

When making this salad, your potatoes can be peeled or used with the peel on. I like Yukon Gold potatoes with the peel on. Feel free to use red potatoes or even baking potatoes. I typically peel the baking potatoes.

broccoli casserole

This is my brother John's recipe. Every time I create this casserole I think of him. He died in a car accident in Brussels when I was 28 years old. I know that he would be thrilled that I still make this dish. I am also positive I would have had many other "John" recipes because he loved to cook.
John wasn't perfect, but he was a great big brother!

2 large crowns of broccoli, chopped

1 small onion, chopped

8 ounce mushrooms, finely chopped

1 can cream of mushroom soup

1/2 cup Hellman's mayo

1 tablespoon Worcestershire sauce

1 egg

16 ounces sharp cheddar cheese, shredded

1 sleeve butter crackers, crushed

1/2 teaspoon salt and pepper

1. **Preheat oven to 350 degrees.**
2. **Place all** items in a large bowl. **Mix well.**
3. **Place** in a greased 9 x 13 casserole dish.
4. **Bake for 30 – 40 minutes.**

This dish is outstanding with Roast Chicken and the Potato Casserole.

southern fried chicken

I am a fourth generation Southern girl, I know how to fry chicken and bake biscuits. For the best results, fry your chicken in a cast iron pan. Remember to give the chicken room in the pan, you don't want to crowd the chicken pieces. I use a buttermilk brine to help seal in the juice of the chicken. A Southern Sunday dinner includes a large platter of fried chicken. Always a winner!

whole chicken fryer, cut up

3 cups buttermilk

10 dashes hot sauce

1 bay leaf

Peanut Oil for Frying

2 cups self-rising flour

2 teaspoons salt

2 teaspoons pepper

1 teaspoon garlic powder

2 teaspoons paprika

1. In a large bowl, **place chicken pieces, buttermilk, hot sauce and bay leaf. Marinate** for up to 24 hours. This is an important step to creating moist fried chicken.

2. In a cast iron pan, **place 2 inches of oil.** Heat to 350 degrees.

3. In a large baggie, **add** flour, salt, pepper, garlic and paprika. **Shake** to combine this mixture.

4. **Remove** a chicken piece and **tap off** extra buttermilk. **Coat in flour mixture** in the bag. Make sure it is well coated. **Place on a rack** on a sheet pan for 15 minutes. This allows the coating to adhere to the chicken.

5. Once the oil is hot, **add chicken pieces** with the pretty side down. Do not over crowd the pan. **Cook** dark meat for 13 – 15 minutes and white meat for 10 – 12 minutes. Place on rack or paper towels to drain.

6. To hold chicken until serving, **place on a sheet pan in a 250 degree oven.**

alabama boy blt pizza

This pizza hits all the flavors of the classic BLT sandwich with a little southern twist. I created this pizza one night while playing with different ways to make pizza dough. Dick and I had enjoyed a pizza with lettuce on it several years ago. This pizza is a complete meal. There is beer in the dough, bacon as a topping and a White BBQ sauce to dress greens on top. I love the hot pizza with the cold salad!

Pizza Dough

1/2 cup beer, your choice 'cause you
    will have to drink the rest

1/4 cup warm water

1.5 ounces rapid rise pizza yeast

1 1/2 tablespoon salt

1 tablespoon honey

3 tablespoons olive oil

3 cups all-purpose flour

Toppings

12 ounce can fire roasted tomatoes,
    drained

10 slices smoked bacon

4 ounces Gouda cheese, grated

1 head romaine lettuce, chopped

Alabama White Sauce

1/2 cup mayonnaise

2 tablespoons fresh lemon juice

2 tablespoons red wine vinegar

1/4 teaspoon fresh ground black pepper

1/4 teaspoon salt

To prepare Pizza Dough

1. **Heat beer and water** to 110 degrees. In a mixer with dough hook, **add warm liquid, salt, yeast, 2 tablespoons olive oil and honey**. Blend for 2 minutes. **Slowly add flour**. Once flour is completed incorporated allow mixer to **work dough for 5 – 8 minutes. Add** 1 tablespoon olive oil to a large mixing bowl. **Remove** dough. **Place** in oiled bowl. **Coat all sides of the dough** with oil. **Place in warm area**, covered, for 1 1/2 hours.
2. After the dough has risen, **preheat the oven to 400 degrees.**
3. **Fry bacon** until crispy. **Drain** on a paper towel. **Remove** bacon drippings from pan.
4. **Divide dough** into 4 equal parts. With finger tips or rolling pin, **flatten dough** into thin rounds. Over medium heat, in the same pan that you fried the bacon, **cook each dough round**, 2 minutes on each side. You want each side browned but you are not trying to cook the dough all the way through. Transfer to a baking sheet or pizza stone.

To layer Pizza

1. **Spread a thin layer** of fire roasted tomatoes on each dough round.
2. **Sprinkle** an ounce of Gouda cheese on each round.
3. **Chop bacon** and evenly distribute over each pizza.
4. **Place pizzas** in the preheated oven for 13 minutes to melt cheese and complete the baking of the dough.
5. While pizza is cooking, **mix together Alabama white sauce** by combining all ingredients until smooth.
6. In a mixing bowl, **place** the chopped Romaine lettuce. **Lightly dress** the lettuce. (Additional white sauce will remain; can be served on the side).
7. **Allow pizza to cool** for 5 minutes, and then **evenly divide lettuce with dressing across each pizza**. Cut and serve with remaining white sauce as desired!

squash pudding

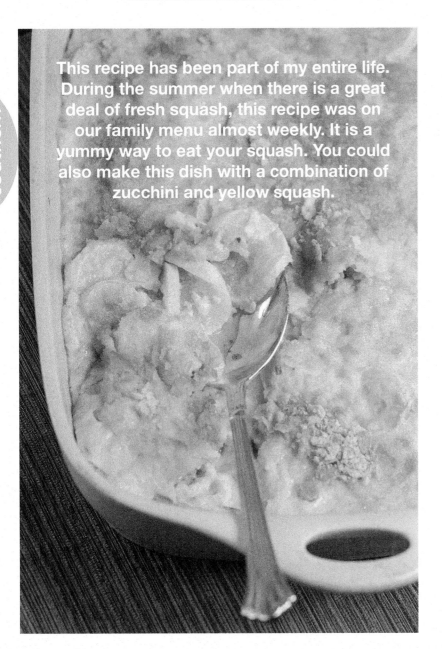

This recipe has been part of my entire life. During the summer when there is a great deal of fresh squash, this recipe was on our family menu almost weekly. It is a yummy way to eat your squash. You could also make this dish with a combination of zucchini and yellow squash.

4 medium yellow squash, sliced into rounds

1 small onion, grated

3 eggs, beaten

1/3 cup milk

2 teaspoons salt

1 can cream of celery soup

15 butter crackers, crumbled

2/3 stick butter

1. **Preheat oven to 350 degrees.**
2. **Cook** squash and onions in a sauce pan with just enough water to cover them until slightly tender. **Drain well**.
3. **Whisk** together eggs, milk, salt and soup in a large bowl.
4. **Add** cooked squash and onions and gently **mix** together.
5. **Melt** butter in a 9 x 13 casserole dish. **Add** squash mixture. **Cover** with crushed crackers.
6. **Cover and bake** 30 minutes at 350 degrees.

cheesy rice

My Mom says she stopped making this dish because one of her children said they didn't like it. I can promise you it wasn't me! This comes together quickly. The dish has crunch from the water chestnuts, creaminess from the cheese and a little warmth from the chilies. To reheat it in the microwave, add a spray of water on the top or place in ice cube into the rice mixture. This helps to steam the rice back into shape.

2 cups Minute Rice

14 ounce can fat free chicken broth

1/3 cup creamy Italian salad dressing

1/2 cup sour cream

1 cup green chilies, diced

1 can sliced water chestnuts, chopped

8 ounces Monterey Jack cheese, shredded

1. **Preheat** oven to 325 degrees.
2. **Cook** Minute rice in chicken broth as directed.
3. **Stir in** remaining ingredients.
4. **Pour** into medium buttered casserole dish.
5. **Bake** for 30 minutes or until bubbly.

sweet potato casserole

The week before Thanksgiving I prepare two pans of this casserole. One is for Thanksgiving and the other is for Christmas dinner. I freeze the second one before cooking. This dish is always part of the menu for the holidays. It doesn't matter if we are also serving a mashed potato casserole. I've also learned you don't mess with this recipe. One year my Aunt Sue and I decided to add orange zest. We were almost kicked out of the family!!

3 cups cooked sweet potatoes, mashed

1/2 cup sugar

2 eggs, beaten

1/2 teaspoon salt

4 tablespoons butter, melted

1/2 cup milk

1 1/2 teaspoons vanilla extract

1/2 cup brown sugar

1/3 cup all-purpose flour

1 cup pecans, chopped

3 tablespoons butter, melted

1. In a large pot, **add sweet potatoes and cover with water**. Don't worry about peeling them before you cook them. The peels will come off very easily after cooking.

2. **Combine** cooled peeled potatoes, sugar, eggs, salt, 4 tablespoons of butter, milk, and vanilla extract in a bowl and mix well.

3. **Spoon into** a 1 to 2 quart baking dish.

4. **Combine** brown sugar, flour, nuts, and 3 tablespoons melted of butter. Sprinkle over potato mixture.

5. **Bake** at 350 degrees for 35 to 40 minutes.

black eyed peas

My New Year's Day meal consisted of baked ham, turnip greens, rice, biscuits, chopped onion, deviled eggs and black-eyed peas. The turnip greens had to be eaten so we would have cash during the year. Black-eyed peas represent good luck. I was simply grateful for the ham, biscuits and deviled eggs as a child. Mix these peas with rice, onions and a little hot pepper sauce and you have a really great dish with your New Year's Day ham.

1 bag of dried black eyed peas,
    soaked in water for 12 hours

6 cups of water

4 - 8 ounces of fat back,
    salt pork or slab bacon

1 teaspoon salt

1/2 teaspoon pepper

1 teaspoon sugar

1. The night before cooking, **soak the black eyed peas** in water for 12 hours. **Drain and discard** the water from the peas.
2. **In a crock pot place the peas and add 6 cups of fresh water. Add the remaining ingredients.**
3. **Cook** the peas on low for 6 hours.
4. **Serve** with rice, chopped onion and hot sauce on New Years Day.

watson's turnip greens

Watson White was a great man and my stepfather. He served as a State and Superior court judge during his long life. He grew up on a farm, fought in World War II and cared for me like I was his own child. If I had to pick a food that reminds me the most of Watson it would be turnip greens because he loved them. His friends would bring him turnip greens by the 30 gallon trash bag. Mom would wash them in the washing machine! Cooking them would put turnip green smell in every inch of the house. Watson didn't care. Give him some warm cornbread, an onion and a glass of buttermilk with his turnip greens and he was a super happy man.

2 large bags pre-washed turnip or collard greens

8 - 12 ounces of fat back or streak-o-lean

1 tablespoon salt

1 teaspoon pepper

1 tablespoon sugar

3 tablespoons apple cider vinegar

1. In a very large pot, **add greens and cover with water.**
2. **Add** remaining ingredients.
3. **Bring to a boil. Reduce heat and cook** on medium low for 2 - 3 hours until greens are tender.

Baked ham is the perfect side dish for the Black Eyed Peas, Spicey Cornbread and Turnip Greens recipes.

my buttermilk biscuits

Making a great biscuit is like learning to ride a bike. It takes practice to understand how it works and once you've learned the process you never forget. I have practiced making these biscuits so much that I do not need measuring cups or a recipe. I just know how it "feels' so that it will come out right. When I teach others to make these biscuits, I teach them by feel as well. If you don't keep buttermilk on hand I have given you an easy substitute.
Biscuits are the best hot and buttered!

1 cup whole milk

3 Tablespoons white distilled vinegar or

apple cider vinegar   OR

1 cup buttermilk

3 cups self-rising flour,

   plus more for kneading

   (I prefer White Lily or King Arthur Flour)

1 1/2 teaspoons salt

2 sticks unsalted butter, frozen

Butter For Brushing and pan

1. **Preheat the oven to 425 degrees.** Biscuits should be cooked in a hot oven.

2. **If you do not have buttermilk**, mix milk and vinegar together in a measuring cup. Let sit for 5 minutes. This gives you the same qualities of regular buttermllk.

3. In a large bowl, **add flour and salt. Grate butter** into the bowl. **Coat butter** with the flour. **Add 3/4 of the buttermilk. Mix** with your hands until the mixture just starts to come together. Be gentle with the mixture. I tell students to treat it like a baby.

4. **Dump** the crumbly mixture on the counter. Keep a small mound of extra flour nearby. You may need it to coat your hands or to add to the mixture if it is too sticky.

5. This next part is very important. **Bring the dough together** into a square shape. Then book or fold the dough eight times. The dough will start to come together as it is booked.

6. **Pat the dough** with your hands until about 1 inch thick. Using a round cutter, **cut straight down**. Don't turn the cutter. This will seal your biscuit and it won't rise. Get as many cuts as you can the first time. Take remaining dough and book it 3 - 4 times. Pat out again and cut.

7. Use a cake pan. **Place 1/2 stick of butter in pan. Melt butter** in the oven. When placing the biscuits in the pan, **coat them on both sides** with the melted butter. Biscuits should be touching in the pan.

8. **Bake for 15 - 18 minutes**. Be careful not to over cook. No one wants a dry biscuit!

nancy's southern stuffing

Mom makes this in huge batches for Thanksgiving. She freezes half so that we have some for Christmas and New Year's Day as well. This can be used as stuffing. Typically we have this in a casserole dish, making this dressing instead of stuffing. Serve with the Giblet Gravy and a slice of turkey. This is Holiday dinner heaven!

3 cups of self-rising cornmeal mix

2 sticks butter, melted

6 eggs, beaten

1/2 cup chopped celery

1 large onion, chopped

1/2 teaspoon salt

1/2 teaspoon black pepper

1 teaspoon fresh sage, finely chopped

1/2 teaspoon marjoram

1/2 teaspoon onion powder

1 1/2 cans chicken broth

1. **Preheat oven to 375 degrees.**
2. In a large bowl **combine** the cornmeal, butter, eggs, celery, onion and seasonings.
3. **Add** the chicken broth until the mixture is thick like a cake batter.
4. **Place** the mixture in a 9 x 13 casserole pan.
5. **Bake for one hour.**
6. This freezes very well.

Variation: Add cooked and crumbled breakfast sausage to this recipe.

dunbutters

Thank you to Floy, my stepmother, for a delicious roll recipe. I can not tell you how many times I have used this recipe. These rolls are super easy, delicious and simple to change. To change the flavor add 2 teaspoons of Italian Seasonings or 2 grated garlic cloves or 2 teaspoons of pesto to change the flavor. You could always create a cheese version as well by adding 1/2 cup of shredded cheddar cheese!

2 cups Bisquick

1 cup butter, melted

1 cup sour cream

1. **Preheat oven to 350 degrees.**
2. In a medium bowl, **add all ingredients and mix thoroughly**.
3. **Spoon** into greased muffin tins. I like to use an ice cream scoop. If there can be portion control around a roll, this is it.
4. **Bake for 15 minutes**.
5. No need for butter. These rolls done been buttered! (English teachers look away from that sentence)!

potato casserole

Here is a potato casserole that has been around for decades. I am sharing the version my family creates. What a glorious potato casserole! It is creamy, cheesy potato goodness! This recipe does freeze well after you bake it off. If you freeze uncooked fresh potatoes, they will turn black and that is not pretty.

2 pound bag cubed potatoes, frozen

1/2 cup butter, melted

1/2 cup onions, chopped

8 ounces cheddar cheese, grated

16 ounces sour cream

1 can cream of chicken soup

salt and pepper to taste

1. **Preheat oven to 375 degrees.**
2. **Thaw potatoes** for nearly an hour.
3. **Mix everything** together in large bowl.
4. **Bake for 45 minutes.**

Great make ahead dish, reheats well.

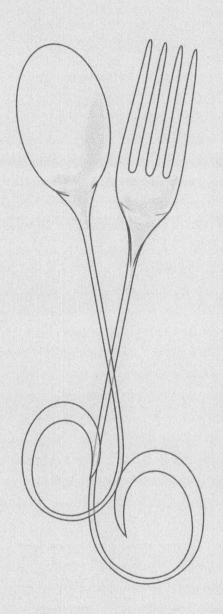

company's coming

bacon wrapped delights

I can't remember how I started to make bacon wrapped anything. Bacon is a great food item. These bacon wrapped delights are exactly as the title says, delightful. Always make more than you think you will need. They are good warm or at room temperature. I am giving you three versions. My Aunt Louise would marinate her dates for 24 hours, so I have tweaked my version to include this unique flavor and technique.

1 1/2 cups brown sugar

1/2 teaspoon cinnamon

1/4 teaspoon nutmeg

1/8 teaspoon salt

1/2 cup orange juice

1/2 cup water

3 tablespoons red wine vinegar or

   white wine vinegar

1 package of regular bacon

   (cherrywood smoked, applewood, or any flavor,

   but save your thick cut bacon for another recipe)

1 can pineapple chunks

2 cups whole pitted dates

4 ounce cream cheese

25 Marcona almonds

Steak Seasoning or BBQ Rub or Chinese 5 Spice

1. **Whisk** brown sugar, cinnamon, nutmeg and salt in a sauce pan. **Add** orange juice, water and vinegar. **Bring to a boil. Reduce heat and simmer** for 5 minutes. **Place dates** in a medium bowl. **Pour** orange juice mixture over dates. **Cover and refrigerate** for 24 hours to develop the best flavor.

2. **Preheat oven to 400 degrees.**

3. **Cut bacon** in half or thirds based on the length. You need enough bacon to wrap each piece once. You want the bacon to over lap about 1/4 of an inch.

4. **Cut pineapple in half. Cut dates in half** lengthwise.

5. Place a piece of bacon on your work surface.
For version #1: Add a piece of pineapple and one half of a date. Roll. Place seam side down on a baking sheet with a rack. **For Version #2**: Add a small cut of cream cheese and an almond. Roll. Place seam side down on the baking sheet with a rack. **Version #3**: Place a whole piece of date on the bacon. Roll. Place seam side down on baking rack.

6. **Sprinkle with** steak seasoning, BBQ seasoning or Chinese 5 Spice seasoning. Or mix and match!

7. **Bake for 20 minutes.** Remember to make twice as many as you think you will need because these go FAST! This is a great appetizer or snack!

cheese olive puffs

As an adult I have learned to love olives and I have always enjoyed cheese. In fact my brother, John, used to say that food is simply a vehicle for cheese. This appetizer is a great vehicle for cheese and I agree. I never find leftovers of this appetizer at any gathering.

1/4 cup butter, room temperature

1/4 teaspoon salt

1/2 cup flour

1/2 teaspoon cayenne pepper

1/2 teaspoon paprika

30 large pitted green olives,
   drained overnight

4 ounces cheddar cheese, grated

1. In a bowl **combine** butter, salt, flour, cayenne pepper and paprika.
2. Using a small ice cream scoop, **create a small ball. Press hole** in ball for olive and **seal the dough around the olive.**
3. **Chill in refrigerator** for several hours or freeze them for about 45 minutes. **Do not skip this step** or the coating will melt off of the olives.
4. **Place them** on a parchment lined baking sheet.
5. **Cook at 400 degrees for 10 – 15 minutes.**
6. **Serve** with homemade mayonnaise with grated garlic.

roasted garlic sauce

I love garlic. Give me garlic, bacon and chocolate and I am super happy. This creamy garlic sauce has been in my recipe box for decades! A good garlic sauce recipe has so many uses. Marinate mushrooms in it. Mix with butter for a great garlic bread spread. Spread on meats before grilling. The possibilities are endless. I also like it because it keeps for weeks in the refrigerator.

30 - 40 garlic cloves, peeled

2 tablespoons balsamic vinegar or sherry vinegar

1/2 cup sour cream (reduced fat or regular)

2 tablespoons fresh basil

2 tablespoons fresh thyme

1/2 to 1 teaspoon horseradish
   (varies based on your like or love of this ingredient)

Pinch salt and pepper

1. **To roast the garlic: Place 30 - 40 cloves of peeled garlic** on a piece of aluminum foil. **Drizzle with olive oil.** Sprinkle with salt and pepper. Close the foil. **Bake at 350 degree for 45 minutes.**
2. **Place all ingredients** in a food processor. **Blend** until combined. **Taste** for salt and pepper adjustments as needed.
3. Now you have to decide how to use it. Some days a piece of crusty bread is all you need. You can use this as a vegetable dip, marinade for poultry, meats and fish or as a pasta sauce.

greek salad

Jimmy the Greek's restaurant was located on the Marietta Square when I was growing up and eating dinner there was the best! This is where I learned that buttery escargot is best with crusty bread for sopping. Jimmy also taught me that potato salad is really yummy under the ingredients for a Greek Salad. I grew up believing this is how a Greek Salad was supposed to be made.

This is my version. You will want to add this to your weekly schedule of foods. That's right, weekly. It is just that good! Potato Salad makes a great side all by itself for lunch and dinner or, if you are Dick Weaver, as an afternoon snack.

For the potato salad:

1 pound red skin potatoes

1 green onion, diced

2 tablespoons mayonnaise

1 tablespoon Greek vinaigrette

Salt and pepper to taste

Greek vinaigrette

1/4 cup red wine vinegar

1 tablespoon Dijon mustard

2 teaspoons dried or fresh oregano, minced

1/2 cup extra virgin olive oil

Salt and pepper to taste

For the salad:

4 - 5 cups Romaine lettuce, spring mix, arugula

1 bell pepper, diced

1 cucumber, diced

2 medium tomatoes, diced

2 beets, diced

4 pepperocini, sliced

16 kalamata olives

3 green onion, diced

1 block feta cheese, crumbled

fresh cracked pepper, to taste

6 anchovies (optional)

1. **Start by making the potato salad. Dice the potatoes** into one inch cubes, then add to a pot of water, **bring to a boil** and cook until fork tender, about 12-15 minutes. **It is important not to over cook the potatoes.** They can become very mushy and fall apart in the potato salad. **Drain the water** and set potatoes aside to cool completely.

2. While the potatoes are cooking, **make the vinaigrette.** You can **place all ingredients** in a blender and process until smooth or put in a bowl and blend with an immersion blender.

3. **When potatoes are cool, mix them** with the green onions, mayonnaise, and 1 tablespoon of Greek vinaigrette. Add salt and pepper to taste. **Place potato salad** in the refrigerator to cool for at least one hour.

4. Makes enough for about 6 salad servings.

5. **To assemble the salad, mix lettuce/spring mix/arugula** in a bowl or on a plate. **Top with bell pepper, cucumber, tomatoes, beets, pepperocini, Kalamata olives, green onions, and sprinkle with feta cheese.** Top with an **anchovy** for an added treat. The potato salad can either be served on the side, on top, or on the bottom of the salad, depending on preference. I serve it under the salad. Add fresh cracked pepper and Greek vinaigrette; enjoy!

company

beefy burger

My brother and sisters are very familiar with this recipe. My Mom made this very often as we were growing up. I have changed the recipe slightly over the years. I found the addition of the mushrooms and red wine made this burger very special. I hope your family falls in love with the tangy sauce and super moist burgers.

2 pounds ground beef, (I prefer 80/20 ground beef)

1 teaspoon salt

1/2 teaspoon black pepper

1 tablespoon Worcestershire sauce

1 teaspoon garlic powder

2 teaspoons butter

8 ounces mushrooms, sliced

1 medium red onion, sliced

2 garlic cloves, minced

1/2 cup red wine

1/2 cup vinegar based BBQ sauce

1. In a medium bowl, **combine the beef, salt, pepper, Worcestershire and garlic powder**. Mix together with your hands until just combined. **Form 6 hamburger patties.**

2. **Heat a cast iron skillet. Add the burgers. Cook** for 6 minutes on the first side and 3 minutes on the second side. Remove the burgers from the pan.

3. **Add the butter** to the pan. Once it is melted **add the mushrooms, onions and garlic. Saute** these ingredients until they are soft.

4. **Add** the wine and reduce by half. **Add** the BBQ sauce.

5. **Return the burgers** to the pan and cook for another 10 minutes.

You can serve these burgers with Mac n Cheese and a salad.

chicken cordon bleu

This recipe was served by everyone on both sides of my family early in my life. What a great dish with a super creamy sauce! Vermouth is not just for cocktails. This dish is even delicious without the sauce. Chicken Cordon Bleu sounds difficult and very fancy. It is not and you can plate it beautifully for an elegant meal or even turn this into a casserole.

8 chicken tenders

1 sleeve butter crackers

1/2 cup grated Parmesan cheese

4 slices boiled ham

4 ounces Monterey cheese, sliced

1/2 cup milk

2 tablespoons all-purpose flour

1/4 cup olive oil

1/4 cup unsalted butter

14 ounce can chicken broth

1/2 cup dry vermouth

1. **Flatten chicken tenders** between two sheets of waxed paper or plastic wrap, using a meat mallet.

2. **Place crackers** in food processor and process crackers into a coarse meal. **Combine with Parmesan cheese** and place in a medium bowl.

3. **Place chicken**, pretty side down, on a cutting board. **Cut ham** in pieces the same size as the chicken. **Place on** chicken pieces.

4. **Slice cheese** into 1/4" pieces. **Place cheese** on top of ham on the smallest end.

5. **Roll the chicken** around the cheese and secure with toothpicks.

6. **Put milk** in a small bowl. **Dip chicken** in the milk and then **coat with** cracker cheese crumbs. **Place** on a plate.

7. **Heat** oil-butter mixture in a skillet and **brown chicken**, carefully turning with tongs; continue until chicken is cooked. **Remove chicken** to a platter.

8. **Add flour** to skillet and stir to **mix with oil** and bits from the chicken. **Pour the broth and the vermouth** into skillet and whisk vigorously. When thickened, **return chicken to the skille**t and coat with sauce. Cut the heat to low to keep things warm until served.

9. **Serve** over rice or egg noodles.

a Southern Legacy

blue cheese dressing

I remember discovering homemade blue cheese dressing with my Dad.
He made a version of this dressing very often when I was in high school.
It is so thick, creamy and tart. It helps to complete the perfect wedge salad.
Just use a wedge of iceberg lettuce, crumbled bacon, diced red onion and
diced tomatoes and this dressing is all you need for salad heaven.

1 cup Hellman's Mayonnaise
(don't substitute)

4 ounce blue cheese, divided

8 ounces sour cream

1/4 cup lemon juice

1 tablespoon Worcestershire Sauce

2 cloves garlic, grated

1/2 teaspoon salt

1/2 teaspoon white or black pepper

2 teaspoons poppy seeds

1. **Place all ingredients, except poppy seeds
   and half of the blue cheese**, in a food processor. Process until smooth. Transfer to a bowl.

2. **Crumble in** remaining blue cheese and **stir in**
   poppy seeds. Chill until serving.

*You can use this as a dip for Buffalo wings
or to make the wedge salad. This lasts for
about 2 weeks in the refrigerator.*

roast chicken

Everyone should know how to roast a chicken. Once you understand the basics, you can change the seasoning or the fat, to make a totally new dish. I teach new brides and teens how to roast a chicken whenever possible. I developed this version after teaching many students how to roast a chicken. This version takes slightly less time to cook because you will remove the back bone before roasting. I save the back bone in the freezer and make chicken stock with it later.

1 whole chicken

1 lemon, cut into quarters

1 carrot, chopped

2 ribs celery, chopped

6 garlic cloves

1 onion

1 stick salted butter

salt

pepper

1. **Preheat oven to 400 degrees.**
2. Remove chicken from package. **Rinse and dry** the chicken. **Cut out** the chicken back.
3. On sheet pan **place thick sliced lemon, carrot, celery, garlic cloves and onion. Place dry chicken,** with breasts up, on vegetables.
4. **Smear** chicken with butter. Generously **salt and pepper**.
5. **Place chicken** in oven for 15 minutes. Then **baste chicken** and lower temp to 350 degrees. For the next hour, **baste the chicken every 10 – 15 minutes.** This is a very important step.
6. The **internal temp of the chicken should be 150 degrees**. Once reached, **remove the chicken** from the oven. Lightly **cover with foil** and allow to rest for 15 minutes before serving.
7. **To make a wonderful gravy, place all** of the roasted chicken juices and vegetables (minus the lemons) in a blender. **Blend** until smooth. **Add water** as needed for consistency. **Serve** on the side as a sauce, or over the chicken or side items such as mashed potatoes.

Variations: Substitute bacon fat or duck fat for the butter. This will change the flavor of the chicken and the sauce. You can also drape the chicken with raw bacon and then roast the chicken. Add herbs based on the season to change the chicken's flavor. Rosemary or sage will make you think of winter. Tarragon is a nice summer herb.

chicken cacciatore

A recipe from my Mom's recipe box. Chicken Cacciatore is a classic and layered with flavor. You will enjoy the end results from the recipe because you are braising the chicken in these lovely flavors and braising creates a very tender result. Your left overs are awesome and increase in flavor. Before packing up left overs go ahead and shred the chicken, place over your rice and add the sauce.
This will help in the reheating process.

2 teaspoons cooking oil

2 medium onions,
   cut in 1/4 inch slices

2 cloves garlic, minced

2 - 3 pounds bone in,
   skin on chicken,
   cut into pieces

16 ounce can diced tomatoes

8 ounce can tomato sauce

1 teaspoon salt

1 teaspoon dried oregano or
   basil, crushed

1/2 teaspoon celery seed

1/4 teaspoon pepper

2 bay leaves

1/2 cup dry white wine

White rice, hot and cooked

1. In a large Dutch oven **heat the cooking oil, add the sliced onions and minced garlic. Cook over a medium heat** until the onions are tender, but not brown, stirring occasionally.

2. Using a slotted spoon **remove the cooked onion slices and garlic from the skillet.** Transfer to a bowl and set aside while cooking the chicken.

3. **Rinse chicken** pieces and pat dry. **Add more cooking oil** to the skillet, if needed, to make about 2 tablespoons. **Add chicken** pieces to skillet, with meaty parts toward the center of the pan where the heat is most intense. **Cook** over medium heat for 15 minutes, turning with tongs as necessary to brown evenly.

4. When the chicken pieces are well-browned, use a large spoon to **return the cooked onions and garlic to the skillet.**

5. In a bowl, **combine** the undrained tomatoes, tomato sauce, salt, oregano or basil, celery seed, pepper and bay leaves. **Pour mixture** over chicken and onions in skillet. **Cover and simmer** over low heat for 30 minutes.

6. **Stir in the white wine. Cook chicken** pieces, uncovered, over low heat 15 minutes longer or until tender, turning occasionally.

7. Chicken is done when it feels tender and is easily pierced with a fork. **Test the thigh or breast at a point near the bone**, as these parts require the most cooking time. Don't be concerned if the meat nearest the bone darkens or still is pink after cooking. This coloring is caused by natural reactions which occur as the chicken cooks, and does not affect flavor.

8. Use a wide, shallow spoon to **skim the fat** from the skillet. The fat is the oily looking part of the liquid that rises to the top.

9. **Remove bay leaves. Transfer chicken** and sauce to a serving dish.

10. **Serve with hot cooked rice.**

a Southern Legacy

chicken kiev

The best trick you can accomplish in this recipe it to keep the butter "safe" inside of the rolled chicken. Cutting into the chicken and having butter run onto the plate is wonderful. Feel free to change up the herbs in the butter and add red pepper flakes or cayenne pepper if you like spicier food. If you are going to deep fry the chicken, you could wrap the chicken in bacon. I mean why not?

4 boneless, skinless chicken breasts

Salt, pepper and mace to taste

1/2 pound butter

2 tablespoons chives, minced

2 teaspoons parsley, minced

2 tablespoons lemon juice

2 eggs

1/2 cup all-purpose flour

Bread crumbs

1. **Mix together** the butter, chives, parsley, and lemon juice. Shape into a roll and place in the refrigerator to harden. Then cut into 8 pieces and put one piece in each chicken breast.

2. **To prepare each chicken breast, cut them in half** to make 2 flat pieces. Then pound between pieces of waxed paper or plastic wrap until very thin.

3. **Season with** the salt, pepper, and mace.

4. **Roll up chicken** making sure to encase the butter. Secure with toothpicks.

5. **Beat two eggs** with 2 tablespoons of water. **Dip chicken** rolls into egg mixture, roll in flour, and then in bread crumbs.

6. **Bake** in a shallow pan (ungreased) at 450 degrees for 20 – 30 minutes until browned.

7. As **an alternative** you can dip in egg mixture, rolled in flour and bread crumbs and then **fried in deep fat fryer** until golden brown.

8. **Serve** with a loaded baked potato and a Caesar salad.

tournedos royale

My Mother, Dad and Grandmother created some wonderful beef dishes.
I have relied on them to teach me how to prepare this expensive but amazing cut
of meat. This dish is elegant. I love the ease of this dish and the ending sauce.
A beef fillet should never be cooked beyond medium rare.

company

6 strips bacon

6 beef fillets about 1 1/2" thick

6 garlic cloves, minced

Black pepper, to taste

1 can condensed golden mushroom soup

1/3 cup Madeira wine

1 tablespoon finely chopped shallots

6 tablespoons brandy

large flake salt (Maldon, Grey or Kosher)

1. **Wrap bacon** around the outer edge of the fillet. Fasten with toothpicks. **Rub meat** with garlic and sprinkle with black pepper. **Broil** for 4 minutes on the first side. **Turn and broil** another 4 minutes.

2. In a sauce pan, **combine soup, Madeira and shallots**. Heat until bubbly.

3. **Place Filets** on a platter. **Drizzle with brandy** and flambé. **Sprinkle** each filet with salt. **Spoon** soup mixture over fillets for service. **Serving suggestions** include Pretty Potatoes and Ginger Glazed carrots.

rice & mushrooms

I remember this recipe as a side item on Christmas Eve at my Grandmother's house. I attribute the recipe to my stepmother, Floy. This has really straight forward ingredients and cooks in the oven. When you are entertaining it is important to have recipes that taste great and don't require a great deal of attention to complete.

1 cup long grain regular rice

3/4 stick butter

1 can chicken broth

1 can onion soup (not cream)

8 ounces mushrooms, sliced

1. In a sauce pan, **brown rice** in butter. **Add** the remaining ingredients and stir.
2. **Pour this mixture** into a 9 x 13 casserole pan. **Mix well** and cover with aluminum foil.
3. **Bake at 325 degrees for 1 hour.**
4. This dish can be made ahead. When ready to reheat, add 2 ice cubes and cover with foil. This reheating method helps to steam the rice. Place in a 350 degree oven for 15 minutes.

asian beef short ribs

with Coconut Rice and Sugar Snap Peas

Variation: The ribs can be made in a Dutch oven or slow cooker.
Using these methods will require a much longer cooking time. Brown your ribs in a sauce pan.
Follow the pressure cooking layering instruction but use your Dutch Oven. Cook at 300 for 5 hours.

a Southern Legacy

I created this recipe early in my personal chef career. I made it in an electric pressure cooker. That is how I fell in love with an electric pressure cooker. Everything for the ribs can be made in this one pot. The cooking time is much shorter. The results are nothing less than perfection! My husband tells everyone we meet about this recipe. It is a great dinner party dish. I enjoy the great beef flavor, creamy rice and the crunch of the sugar snap peas.

For the Ribs

3 pounds beef short ribs

3/4 cup all-purpose flour

1 tablespoon olive oil

1 large onion, sliced

4 garlic cloves, chopped

1 teaspoon salt

1 teaspoon pepper

1 cup sake

1/2 cup Hoisin sauce, divided

For Rice and Sugar Snap Peas

1 can coconut milk

1 cup water

1 1/2 cups Arborio rice

1/2 teaspoon salt

1 1/2 cups sugar snap peas

1. **In a bowl or large plastic baggie, place short ribs. Add** flour, salt and pepper. Shake or toss to **coat the ribs.**

2. If using an electric pressure cooker, set to "browning" or saute' to heat. If using a standard pressure cooker simply preheat. Once hot, add oil. **Brown ribs** on all sides in batches. You are just looking to get a good caramelization on each side.

3. **Remove ribs** from pressure cooker. **Add half the onion slices** and half of the garlic. **Place half the ribs on the onions,** meaty side down. **Add remaining onions and garlic. Add remaining ribs and salt and pepper.**

4. **Pour** in sake. **Drizzle** 1/2 of the hoisin sauce. Place lid on cooker. Set electric pressure cooker to **high pressure for 30 minutes. Let sit for 10 minutes** and manually release the steam. If using a standard pressure cooker, set a timer for 30 minutes and then wait 10 minutes to release the pressure. Press start. Once timer is done, wait 10 minutes to release the pressure. In the meantime, **place coconut milk, water, rice and salt** in a large saucepan. **Bring to a soft boil. Cover and reduce** heat to medium low. **Stir** rice mixture every 5 minutes. **After 15 minutes add the sugar snap peas.** Turn off heat in 5 minutes.

5. **Serve with** rice and sugar snap peas on the base of the plate. Top with Ribs. Green onions or sliced sugar snap peas may be used as a garnish with the remaining hoisin sauce.

marinated flank steak

This recipe represents my first original recipe and the first time to really work hard to get a recipe perfect. It is an easy week night recipe that looks like a special occasion. I have to admit when I started making this I used canned mushrooms. I have since learned the error of my ways. Please, please eliminate canned mushrooms from your pantry. No one wants little rubbery things in a sauce! If you don't like the mushrooms at all, they are easily omitted. You could add one shallot minced or 1/2 of a red onion sliced.

1/2 cup water

1/4 cup light soy sauce

1/4 cup light brown sugar

1/2 teaspoon ginger, minced

2 garlic cloves, minced

1 (2 – 4 pound) flank steak

1 tablespoon balsamic vinegar

1/4 cup water

8 ounce button mushrooms, sliced

2 teaspoons corn starch

2 tablespoons water

1. **Place first 5 ingredients** in a plastic bag and shake until mixed.

2. **Add flank steak.** Marinate in the refrigerator for 30 minutes to 24 hours, turning occasionally.

3. **Preheat oven to Broil.** You may also cook this on the grill or in a cast iron grill pan.

4. **For the Oven**: Place flank steak on a foil lined pan. Broil the flank steak on the first side for 6 minutes. Flip the steak and broil for another 3 minutes. Remove from the oven. Cover loosely with foil. Let it rest for 15 minutes before slicing.

5. **For the grill:** Heat grill to 450. Place steak on grill for 5 minutes. Flip and give it another 3 minutes. Remove to a tray and cover with foil. Allow to rest for 15 minutes before slicing.

6. **For the Grill pan**: Heat the grill pan on your stove top, without any fat, until the pan is smoking hot. Lower the heat to medium high. Add steak. It should sizzle. Cook on the first side for 6 minutes. Turn and cook on the second side for 3 minutes. Move to a platter. Cover with foil. Let it rest for 15 minutes before slicing.

7. **For the sauce, pour the marinade** into a sauce pan and put on medium low heat. While the steak is cooking, **add** the vinegar, additional water and mushrooms to the marinade. **Bring to a boil. Mix corn starch and water** together to create a slurry. **Add** to sauce pan and reduce heat to low. **Stir** until thickened.

8. **Cut the steak** in thin slices against the grain of the meat. **Serve with sauce.**

beef wellington

What an elegant dish! When I mention Beef Wellington to a client their eyes light up. Beef Wellington combines so many delicious items. I am a pate' lover. It is creamy and has such a distinct flavor. When you combine that with earthy mushrooms, shallots and butter you create a great bite. When I get to pick a cut of beef, it will always be a fillet. This dish then takes that wonderful fillet and adds a crust. Entree happiness for sure!

1 whole filet of beef, trimmed

1/4 cup melted butter

4 ounces liver pate'

1 tablespoon shallot, minced

3 tablespoons mushrooms,
   finely chopped

2 sheets of puffed pastry

1/4 cup cold unsalted butter

1/2 cup ice water

1 egg, well beaten

1. **Preheat oven to 400 degrees.**

2. **Shape filet** into a long, even roll, turning under long narrow ends and tying them into place with cotton twine. **Place in a roasting pan** and brush with melted butter. **Roast in a pre-heated hot oven at 400 degrees for 20 minutes**. **Remove** from oven and cool. **Remove** the cotton twine.

3. **Mash** liver pate and **stir in** shallots and mushrooms. **Spread** liver mixture over cooled filet.

4. **Roll out** one fourth of the pastry on a floured board into an oblong shape large enough to enclose the filet. **Place filet**, liver-coated side down, in the middle of the crust. **Wrap crust** around filet and fasten edges with egg. **Fold in ends** and fasten with egg. **Place filet** seam side down on a greased cookie sheet. **Brush with egg.**

5. To add decoration to the top of the pastry, **roll out remaining crust and cut** into 1/2 inch wide strips. **Arrange strips in a crisscross** over filet. **Cut stems, leaves and 1-inch rounds with remaining crust for decorations**. Arrange rounds on top of roll in the shape of a rose. Add stems and leaves. Brush decorations with beaten egg. **Bake in a preheated hot oven (400 degrees) for 25 to 30 minutes** or until richly browned. **Cut with a sharp knife,** using a sawing motion.

6. **Serve** with broiled mushroom crowns, hot cooked peas and baby onions. Garnish with watercress.

lobster thermidor

My Mom was Mrs. Atlanta in 1968. Pretty cool, huh? I was four at the time. I didn't get to go to the pageant. I was, however, in the photograph featured in the paper. When she competed for Mrs. Atlanta it included both homemaking and beauty. My Mom created two recipes for her pageant competition. This is one of them and the other is a rich chocolate cake. The recipe calls for 2 whole lobsters and is rich and delicious. I will tell you that 2 lobster tails per person is a good substitute.

4 (2 pound) lobsters or

   2 lobster tails per person

1/2 pound mushrooms, sliced

4 tablespoons butter

4 tablespoons of all-purpose flour

1/2 teaspoon salt and pepper

Tabasco to taste

1 teaspoon Worcestershire sauce

2 tablespoons cognac

1 pint light cream

1/4 pound freshly grated Parmesan

unseasoned bread crumbs

1/4 cup cheddar cheese

1. **Choose a pot** large enough to hold all your lobsters comfortably; **do not crowd them**. A 4- to 5-gallon pot can handle 6 to 8 pounds of lobster. **Fill with water**, allowingv 3 quarts of water per 1-1/2 to 2 pounds of lobster.

2. **Add 1/4 cup sea salt** for each gallon of water. Bring the water to a rolling boil.

3. **Add** the live lobsters or lobster tails **one at a time,** and start timing immediately. Do not cover.

4. For the live lobsters, **stir the lobsters** halfway through cooking. **Cook for 25 – 30 minutes** once lobsters are in the water. They should be a bright red when done. **Remove from water** and let them cool in the shell. This helps some of the liquid absorb back into the lobster meat.

5. **Cut the lobsters or tails** in half from the top of their heads to their tails. Pull off claws. Remove meat from tail and claws. Chop into 1" pieces. Clean the body shell of the lobster for presentation.

6. **Sauté** sliced mushrooms in butter until soft. **Sprinkle** flour, salt and pepper over mushrooms. **Stir to blend** for 2 minutes. **Add** tabasco, Worcestershire and Cognac. **Stir in** lobster and cream. **Simmer** for 5 minutes. **Add** parmesan cheese.

7. **Place** lobster shells in 9 x 13 casserole dish. **Spoon lobster filling** into each shell. **Top with** breadcrumbs and cheddar cheese. **Broil for 2- 3 minutes.**

8. This is an incredibly rich dish. Serve with a salad and end your meal with the Lemon Fluff! This is a simply elegant meal.

ginger glazed carrots

My husband, Mom and clients love these glazed carrots! It is a zingy, slightly sweet side dish topped with macadamia nuts! Carrots are not only good for you, but add a great pop of color on your plate. Remember we eat with our eyes first!

3/4 cup orange juice

3 tablespoons dark brown sugar

2 tablespoons crystallized ginger, chopped

2 tablespoons butter

1 pound turned/baby carrots

1 clove garlic, minced

salt to taste

white pepper to taste

1/2 cup macadamia nuts

1. In a sauce pan, over medium high heat, **add orange juice, sugar, ginger, butter, garlic and carrots.**

2. **Cook carrots** in this mixture until they are fork tender. With a slotted spoon, **remove carrots** to serving bowl. Continue cooking the liquid until it is a syrup consistency.

3. **Spoon the syrup** over carrots. Sprinkle with salt, white pepper and nuts.

company

sausage stuffed mushrooms

I love making these stuffed mushrooms. My students love learning how to make them. They can be an appetizer or a side dish. There always seems to be extra filling. You can bake the filling in a ramekin and serve as a dip with crackers or corn chips. This dish freezes very well.

12 large button mushrooms

3 scallions, white and green parts, minced

1 garlic clove, minced

1 tablespoon good olive oil

1 1/2 tablespoons brandy

1/2 pound sweet Italian sausage, removed from the casings

1 tablespoon Worcesteshire sauce

1/3 cup Panko crumbs

3 ounces cream cheese

1/4 cup freshly grated Parmesan

1 tablespoon minced fresh parsley leaves

Salt and freshly ground black pepper

1. **Preheat the oven to 350 degrees.**

2. **Remove the stems** from the mushrooms. **Place** the mushrooms stem, green onions and garlic in a food processor. **Pulse** 5 or 6 times.

3. **Place the caps** of the mushrooms in a casserole dish or baking sheet. **Add brandy** to the bottom and let the mushrooms absorb the liquid.

4. Heat a cast iron skillet. **Cook the Italian sausage. Add** olive oil and the mushroom mixture. **Cook** mushrooms until the moisture is gone.

5. **Add** cream cheese, Worcestershire sauce, Panko, salt and pepper. **Mix** until the cream cheese is well combined. **Cool** this mixture slightly. **Combine all.**

6. **Over fill each mushroom** with the filling. **Top** with parmesan cheese and parsley.

7. **Bake for 20 minutes.**

8. **Serve** as an appetizer or as a side dish.

yeast rolls

Yeast rolls are certainly a treat. When I was growing up my family attended Wednesday Night Supper at Church each week. The best part of any meal was the yeast roll with butter. They were light, airy and buttery - the perfect combination. Now I have a version that makes me equally as happy.

3 rapid rise yeast packets

1/2 cup luke warm water

4 tablespoons sugar

1/2 cup lard, Crisco or bacon fat

1 teaspoon salt

1/2 cup boiling water

3 cups all-purpose flour, whisked

Butter for brushing the tops of the rolls

1. **Proof your yeast** in the luke warm water. What is luke warm? Very warm but not hot water. Ever tested milk on your wrist from a baby bottle? That very warm but not hot feel is what you want. **Let this proof for 5 – 10 minutes**. There should be a small amount of foam building on the top to let you know the yeast is active. **Add the sugar** to the yeast mixture and stir.

2. With a whisk, **cream your fat of choice with the salt. Whisk in** boiling water. **Add** proofed yeast mixture.

3. **Add flour**. I recommend working in one cup of flour at a time.

4. **Put your dough mixture into a large bowl**. Wrap with plastic wrap and leave in the **refrigerator over night.** You can actually leave it here for days and just use what you want every day.

5. **Preheat oven to 400 degrees.**

6. **Create 3 inch dough balls** or roll out the dough to 1/2 inch thickness and cut biscuits. Then fold the biscuits in half.

7. **Bake for 14 minutes. Brush with melted butter** as soon as they come out of the oven.

pretty potatoes

As a Personal Chef, food presentation is super important. After all, we eat with our eyes first! The thing I love the most is that once cooked, these are crunchy on the outside and soft and creamy on the inside. A finishing salt is typically a larger flaked salt and sometimes is flavored. Using a finishing salt gives a super salty crunch to the top of the potatoes.

4 large Yukon Gold Potatoes

4 tablespoons butter

4 tablespoons olive oil

2 teaspoons Italian, Greek, or
    steak seasoning

coarse finishing salt
    (like Maldon or Grey salt)

1. **Preheat oven to 400 degrees.**
2. **Fill a large bowl** half way with water. **Peel the potatoes and place in the water.** This helps to keep them from turning brown.
3. With a vegetable peeler, **shave long thin pieces** off of each potato. They should be about an inch wide and 3- 4 inches long. **Place back in the water.**
4. In a bowl, **melt butter and olive oil** together. **Stir in** herbs and spices (except coarse salt),
5. In a muffin tin **place a teaspoon of the butter mixture** in each space.
6. **Start by layering** 3 – 4 slices of the potato overlapping each piece by half of the potato. Continue adding layers until you have **4 – 5 layers**. Using a teaspoon, **place some of the butter mixture** on the potatoes. Starting at one end, **roll up the potatoes. Place in a muffin compartment**. It will resemble a flower. Add slices of potato to the edges as needed to fill. **Spoon more butter mixture** over potatoes if there is any left after all potatoes have been rolled.
7. **Bake for 20 – 30 minutes**. You want a crispy outside and s creamy inside.
8. When plating, **add a generous pinch of Maldon or Grey salt.** This is a great time to use a flavored salt as well.
9. **Serve** with the Marinated Flank Steak.

popovers

1 cup all-purpose flour
1/2 teaspoon salt
1 cup fat milk
   (whole or 2%, you choose)
2 large eggs
1 tablespoon butter, melted
pats of butter

I can remember watching cooking shows on PBS in my thirties. I loved Saturday because it was cooking show day! I thought popovers would be really challenging to create. It turns out they look like they take a great deal of effort, but really are not. I make popovers often. It is an easy dinner bread. You can change the popover flavor easily by adding herbs, garlic or even cheese. For parties, popovers have a wow factor. If you don't have a popover pan, you may use a muffin tin.

1. **Preheat oven to 375°.**
2. **Lightly spoon flour** into a dry measuring cup leveled with a knife. To be honest, this is how you should always measure flour.
3. **Combine flour and salt**, stirring with a whisk.
4. **Combine milk and eggs** in a medium bowl, stirring with a whisk until blended.
5. **Gradually add flour mixture**, stirring well with a whisk. **Stir in butter.** Let stand 30 minutes.
6. **Add a small pat of butter** to each muffin tin slot or in your popover pan slots. Place pan in oven for 5 minutes to **melt the butter** and heat the pan.
7. Using a ladle or measuring cup **divide the batter** into you selected pan.
8. **Bake at 375° for 40 minutes or until golden.**

blue cheese popovers

If you are a blue cheese lover, you will enjoy this popover. I fell in love with popovers decades ago. I decided to add blue cheese and some herbs and create a popover rich enough to stand up next to a great piece of red meat. Yes, popovers are wonderful in a popover pan. However you can make a really decent popover in your muffin tins. There is a bunch of blue cheese flavor in each bite.

2 eggs

1 cup milk, room temp

2 tablespoons butter, melted

1 cup all-purpose flour

1/2 teaspoon salt

1/4 teaspoon pepper

1 ounce crumbled blue cheese

1 tablespoon fresh thyme, chopped

4 pats of butter

1. **Whisk eggs, milk, butter, flour, salt and pepper together** until lumps are gone OR place those ingredients in a blender and process until smooth. **Whisk in cheese and thyme**. Put in airtight container for 2 hours to one day in advance.

2. **Preheat oven to 425 degrees**.

3. You can use a muffin tin or a popover tray. **Cut** 4 pats of butter. **Cut** each of those into fourths. **Place a pat of butter** into each muffin or popover compartment. Put the pan in the preheated oven long enough to **melt the butter,** about 3 minutes.

4. Using a ladle or measuring cup, **fill each compartment 3/4 of the way.**

5. **Bake for 18 – 20 minutes.** These are rich and flavorful. I prefer to serve this with a pot roast or beef fillet.

a Southern Legacy

desserts

blueberry swirl

I can remember how excited I would be if Nanny prepared this for a family gathering. Who am I kidding, I still get excited to see this created or to make it myself. Dick enjoyed this dessert the first time I made dinner for him. Maybe that is why he asked me to marry him!?

1 stick of butter, softened

1 cup pecans, finely chopped

1 cup all-purpose flour

8 ounces cream cheese, softened

1 cup powdered sugar

16 ounce container Cool Whip

1 6.5 ounce package
   of instant vanilla pudding

2 cups milk

1 pint blueberries

1. **Preheat oven to 350 degrees.**
2. With a mixer, **cream butter. Add nuts and flour.** Press into an ungreased 9 x 13 casserole dish.
3. **Bake for 20 minutes.** Remove and cool.
4. **Mix** cream cheese, powdered sugar and 1 cup Cool Whip in a medium bowl until smooth. **Pour over cooled crust.**
5. **Whisk** together pudding and milk. **Fold in** the blueberries. **Spread over** cream cheese mixture.
6. **Spread remaining Cool Whip. Chill and serve.**

chocolate layer dessert

My Nanny lived in Barnesville, Georgia most of the time I knew her as my Nanny. She was a math teacher, master bridge player and a great cook. The recipes we hold dear to us were published in the Barnesville Baptist Cookbook. I treasure the ones I have. It has my Nanny's pencil marking in it where she changed or combined recipes. It is perfect for pot lucks, dinner gatherings and showers. It is so yummy.

1 cup self-rising flour

1 stick unsalted butter, softened

1/2 cup chopped nuts,
    pecans or walnuts

---

8 ounces cream cheese, softened

1 cup powdered sugar

1 large container, Cool Whip, less 1 cup

6 3/4 ounce (large) instant
    chocolate pudding

2 cups milk

1. **Preheat oven to 350 degrees.**
2. **For the crust, combine** the self-rising flour, butter and chopped nuts. Mix well and press in 9 x 13 pan.
3. **Bake for 15 minutes.** Cool completely.
4. **For the next layer, mix** together the cream cheese, powdered sugar and Cool Whip. Remember to leave a cup for the top layer. **Cream well and spread** over cooled crust.
5. **For the third layer combine** instant pudding and milk. **Pour over** the cream cheese layer.
6. **Top with** remaining Cool Whip. **Sprinkle with** chopped pecans.
7. **Refrigerate** until ready to serve.

mrs. atlanta chocolate cake

My Mom was Mrs. Atlanta in 1968. I am very proud of her title. I loved walking around in her crown and sash when I was younger. I suspect this is where my love of a crown came from! When she competed she created this dish. She made it as a Christmas gift for so many people. She used pecans and the red and green jellied candy to make bells on the top. What a great gift to receive!

Cake

1/2 cup Crisco

1 stick unsalted butter, softened

2 cups sugar

4 ounces semi sweet chocolate, melted

2 eggs

2 cups cake flour or 1 3/4 cup all-purpose flour and 1/4 cup cornstarch

1 teaspoon salt

2 teaspoons baking powder

1 1/2 cups whole milk

2 teaspoons vanilla extract

1 cup pecans, finely chopped

1. **Preheat oven to 375 degrees.**
2. In the bowl for your mixer, **beat together** Crisco, butter and sugar for 4 - 5 minutes.
3. **Add** melted chocolate and eggs. **Beat** until combined.
4. In a medium bowl, **add** flour, salt and baking powder. **Whisk together**.
5. **Add 1/3 of the flour** mixture to the mixing bowl. **Add half** of the milk. **Add another third** of the flour. **Add remaining milk. Add remaining flour mixture.** Beat until just combined each time.
6. **Add** vanilla.
7. **Add** pecans.
8. **Butter and flour** two 9" cake pans. Divide batter between the cake pans.
9. **Bake cake rounds for 35 minutes**.
10. **Let cool in pans** for 10 minutes. Remove and cool on baking racks. Cool completely before icing.

Icing

1 stick butter

4 ounces Baker's unsweetened chocolate 100% Cacao

2 eggs

1 box powdered sugar

1 teaspoon vanilla extract

Juice of a half lemon

1. Add 1 inch of water to a sauce pan. Place a metal bowl on the sauce pan. This **creates a double boiler.** Bring water in the sauce pan to a boil. In the metal bowl, **melt chocolate and butter.** Let this cool for 10 minutes.
2. **Beat in the eggs**, one at a time, with a hand mixer.
3. **Whisk the powdered sugar and slowly add** to the chocolate mixture until all is well combined.
4. **Add the vanilla and lemon juice** with the hand mixer. Beat on medium for several minutes.
5. This makes enough icing to frost a two layer cake.

a Southern Legacy

sugar & spice nuts

All Southern girls should be able to create a sweet nut snack for a shower or ladies gathering. When I plan a dinner party, I select three appetizers and a nut or something easy to nibble. Place a bowl of these nuts at the bar or at the front entrance or in the kitchen where everyone gathers. After the party save these nuts as a topping for your favorite salad.

1 cup sugar

1/2 cup water

3/4 teaspoon salt

1 teaspoon cinnamon

1 teaspoon vanilla

1 pound nuts, pecans, walnuts,

peanuts, almonds, cashew…

your choice

1. **Combine all ingredients, except nuts and vanilla,** in a medium to large sauce pan.
2. **Cook** until syrup spins a small thread (about 5 minutes) **remove from heat**. A cooked sugar mixture can go from not doing anything to over cooked really quickly. **Don't walk away during this step.**
3. **Add nuts and vanilla**. The sugar will bubble. **Stir quickly** until crystallized and sugar coats the nuts.
4. **Pour onto** buttered waxed paper or parchment paper.
5. **Cool and separate** nuts and store in a covered tin.

baked egg custard

Certain recipes make you think of particular people. This recipe definitely reminds me of my Dad and his mom, Grandmother Hodges. It is creamy and has an amazing mouth feel. Many people have never experienced an egg custard: which is similar to creme brûlée without the sugar coating. My best friend and her husband enjoyed this dessert in my home countless times. I dedicate this recipe to Bob Aebersold, my best friend's husband, who loved this dish and requested it every time I cooked for him.

1 cup sugar

4 cups whole milk
   (not a time to save calories)

8 eggs

1/2 cup sugar

1 1/2 teaspoons vanilla extract

dash of salt

1. **Preheat oven to 300 degrees.**
2. **To caramelize the sugar** for the bottom of the custard pan, **put 1 cup of sugar** in a small sauce pan. **Warm this** over medium heat. The sugar will begin to melt. **Stir until** the sugar begins to turn a light brown color. **Remove from heat and pour** the hot caramelized sugar into the bottom of a 1 quart casserole dish.
3. In saucepan, **scald milk.** What is this? Heat the milk until just before it boils and then turn off the heat.
4. **Whisk eggs, 1/2 cup sugar, vanilla and salt** in a bowl. You need to temper your eggs. If you pour your eggs directly into the hot milk you run the risk of them cooking. Chunky custard is not yummy. **Temper eggs by adding a half cup scaled milk to egg mixture and whisk.** Once tempered add all of egg mixture to scalded milk.
5. **Pour mixture over** caramelized sugar (you did this in step 2). **Place casserole dish** on a lipped sheet pan. Carefully **pour warm water** in the sheet pan. Bring the water half way up the outside of the casserole dish.
6. **Bake for 1 hour** or until set. **Remove from oven** and let the custard cool on the counter for 30 minutes. Then **cover and refrigerate** until cold.
7. **Unmold to serve.** The caramelized sugar will become liquid and run on the plate. **Garnish with** sliced strawberries or other fresh fruit and fresh whipped crème.

very moist coconut cake

I LOVE cake. I like icing. I love this cake because it doesn't have icing and it is super moist. This recipe is a version of a pound cake, but it is not so dense. Instead you have a moist crumb and great coconut flavor. You could use this cake recipe and the Apple Cake recipe for a buffet dessert and everyone will be happy.

1 1/2 cups shortening or butter
   (or both as long as it equals 1 1/2 cups)
2 1/4 cups sugar
5 eggs
3 cups all-purpose White Lily Flour
   (the brand is important)
1 teaspoon baking powder
1/2 teaspoon salt
1 cup milk
2 teaspoons coconut extract
1 small bag shredded coconut

Syrup
3/4 cup water
1 1/2 cups sugar
2 tablespoons butter
1 1/2 teaspoons coconut extract

1. **Preheat oven to 325 degrees.**
2. In a mixing bowl, **cream shortening/butter and sugar** for 3 - 5 minutes. Add your eggs one at a time. Once they are all added, beat at high speed for 10 minutes.
3. **Whisk flour, baking powder and salt togethe**r in a bowl. **Add flour mixture and milk** mixture alternately. Start and end with flour.
4. **Add** coconut extract and coconut and stir.
5. **Butter and flour** a Bundt pan and **add the batter.**
6. **Bake for 1 hour and 25 minutes.** Allow to cool in the pan until syrup is ready.
7. **To make syrup;** place all syrup ingredients, except extract, in a sauce pan. **Bring to a boil** and cook for 5 minutes. **Remove** from heat. **Add** coconut extract and stir.
8. **Poke holes in the cake** with a wooden skewer. **Pour over** the hot cake. **Let cake cool** completely in the pan. **Turn out. Freeze** before serving. Keep refrigerated.

desserts

bacon bourbon brownies

My love of bacon and chocolate led me to create this recipe. When I tell people I have a Bacon Bourbon Brownie recipe all I hear is "hmmm" and "ooooo". The bacon gives this brownie the salt flavor that goes so well with chocolate. Adding bourbon just takes the whole brownie to another level.

desserts

1/2 cup pecans

1/2 pound sliced bacon,
reserve 3 tablespoons of fat

8 ounces bittersweet chocolate, chopped

2 ounces unsweetened chocolate, chopped

1 stick plus 2 tablespoons unsalted butter

1 cup granulated sugar

1/2 packed cup light brown sugar

3 tablespoons bourbon

4 large eggs

1 teaspoon salt

1/4 cup unsweetened cocoa powder

1 1/2 cups all-purpose flour

1. **Preheat the oven to 350°.** Line a 9-inch square baking pan with parchment paper, allowing 2 inches of overhang on 2 opposite sides. **Spray the paper with vegetable spray.**

2. **Spread the pecans** in a pie plate and **toast** for about 8 minutes, until fragrant. **Let cool, then coarsely chop the nuts.**

3. In a skillet, **cook the bacon** over moderate heat, turning once, until crisp, about 6 minutes. **Drain** on paper towels and let cool; reserve 3 tablespoons of the fat. Finely **chop the bacon.**

4. In a saucepan, **combine both chocolates with the butter and stir** over very low heat, until melted; **scrape into a large bowl.** Using a handheld electric mixer, **beat in both** sugars with the reserved 3 tablespoons of bacon fat. **Beat in** the bourbon. **Add** the eggs and salt and beat until smooth. **Sift** the cocoa and flour into the bowl and beat until blended.

5. **Scrape the batter into** the prepared pan and **sprinkle** the bacon and pecans on top. **Bake for about 50 minutes,** until the brownies are set around the edges but slightly wobbly in the center; a toothpick inserted into the center should have some batter clinging to it. **Transfer the pan** to a rack and let the brownies cool completely. **Lift the brownies** out of the pan using the parchment paper. **Cut** into squares or rectangles and serve.

a Southern Legacy

apple cake with caramel glaze

This cake will become your go to Apple Cake recipe. The cake comes together easily and is super moist. Once you add the caramel glaze the presentation is worthy of an elegant dinner or a gathering of friends. My Nanny made this in the fall. I love that her recipe copy has her pencil markings where she changed the measurements and drew arrows to a different glaze that she preferred for this cake.

2 cups white sugar

1 1/2 cups vegetable oil

2 teaspoons vanilla extract

3 eggs

3 cups all-purpose flour

1 teaspoon baking soda

1/2 teaspoon ground cinnamon

1 teaspoon salt

2 medium Granny Smith apples -
    peeled, cored and diced

1 cup chopped walnuts

For Glaze

1/2 cup butter

2 teaspoons milk

1/2 cup brown sugar

1. **Preheat the oven to 350 degrees. Grease a 9 inch Bundt pan.**
2. In a large bowl, **beat** the sugar, oil, vanilla and eggs with an electric mixer until light and fluffy. This take about 4 minutes.
3. **Combine** the flour, baking soda, cinnamon and salt; stir into the batter just until blended. **Fold in** the apples and walnuts using a spoon. **Pour into** the prepared pan.
4. **Bake for 1 hour and 20 minutes** in the preheated oven, until a toothpick inserted into the crown of the cake comes out clean. **Allow to cool for about 20 minutes** then invert on to a wire rack.
5. **Make the glaze** by heating the butter, milk and brown sugar in a small saucepan over medium heat. **Bring to a boil,** stirring to dissolve the sugar, then remove from the heat. **Drizzle over** the warm cake. I like to place a sheet of aluminum foil under the cooling rack to catch the drips for easy clean up.

caramel cake

Nanny, my Mom's Mom made the best caramel icing ever. We know this because the family requests this treat as often as possible, However we failed to ever get her to write it down. How did we let that happen? My Mom has been determined to recreate her icing based on what she remembered. We have gotten close to it with the assistance of Willie Mae Bramlett. The cake portion of the recipe is mine. I upped the caramel flavor with brown sugar and caramel extract. I hope your family begins to request this cake for every family gathering. Maybe you will even enter it into a Fair Cake Contest and win a blue ribbon. My Nanny certainly did!

1 cup butter, room temperature

1 1/4 cups sugar

3/4 cup light brown sugar

4 eggs, room temperature

1/2 teaspoon vanilla extract

1 teaspoon caramel extract

3 cups all-purpose flour

3 teaspoons baking powder

1 cup buttermilk, room temperature

1. **All ingredients need to be at room temperature**. Feel free to get them out and leave them on the counter the night before you bake.
2. **Preheat oven to 325 degrees.**
3. In a mixing bowl, **cream together butter and sugar** for 5 minutes. **Add eggs** one at a time. (Please crack each egg into a bowl and then add. No one wants eggshells in their cake.) Combine well between each egg.
4. **Add vanilla and caramel extracts. Add flour and milk** alternating. Start with flour and end with flour.
5. You may bake this in (2) 9 inch round pans, a bundt pan or a large rectangular pan.
6. **Bake for 40 - 45 minutes.** Cool for 10 minutes in the pan. Remove from pan and cool completely before icing.

Caramel Icing

3 cups sugar, divided

2 sticks unsalted butter

1 cup whole milk

1 teaspoon vanilla extract

Pinch of salt

1. In a small cast iron skillet, **caramelize 1/2 cup sugar** starting on low heat and increasing to medium heat after the sugar melts. You do not want the sugar to crystallize on the side of your pan. **Stir very gently**. It is ready when it is a medium brown color.
2. In a separate bowl **combine remaining sugar, butter, and whole milk.**
3. **Pour Caramelized Sugar into mixture and whisk**. It will seize up. Don't panic. Keep whisking over the heat and it will melt into the mixture. **Heat in the pan** until it reaches the soft boil stage. (236 degrees if using a candy thermometer)
4. **Add vanilla and a pinch of salt**
5. **Cool to the touch** in a sauce pan. When cooled, moved to the mixing bowl.
6. Use whisk blade in mixer, **whisk 5 to 7 minutes** until creamy

a Southern Legacy

desserts

mrs. betty's rum balls

As a child on Christmas Eve, these Rum Balls were always on a decorative plate on the antique table behind the yellow love seat waiting to be eaten. We were allowed to taste them, but as a child the rum in the balls always ruined the beauty of the powdered sugar covered delight. As an adult the rum is one of the best reason to keep these little balls around! Isn't it interesting how things change as we grow up?!

1 pound vanilla wafer cookies

2 tablespoons cocoa powder

3 tablespoons powdered sugar

3 tablespoons light corn syrup

1 cup walnuts or pecans, chopped

3 jiggers of rum

Powdered sugar for dusting

1. **Place wafers** in your food processor and **crush to a fine crumb**. You may also place the wafers in a large plastic bag and crush them with a rolling pin.

2. In a medium bowl, **combine** the crushed wafers, cocoa, powdered sugar, syrup, nuts and rum.

3. **Roll into** one inch balls. Roll the balls in powdered sugar.

4. **Store** in an air tight container.

date balls

What recipe makes you think of a loved one? A certain holiday? For me, this recipe does both. I connect Date Balls with Christmas. I love the crunch and the sweetness from the dates. The trick is to not get the powdered sugar on your new Christmas Eve dress!

1 stick unsalted butter

8 ounce dates, chopped

1 cup dark brown sugar

1 teaspoon vanilla extract

2 cups rice cereal

1/2 cup to 1 cup chopped nuts, your choice

1/2 cup powdered sugar

1. In a double boiler, **add butter, dates and sugar**. Over low heat cook for 5 minutes stirring often.
2. **Add remaining ingredients** and stir. The mixture should be thick.
3. Using a small ice cream scoop, **create balls** the size of a golf ball.
4. **Roll in powdered sugar.**
5. **Store in airtight container.**

molasses sugar cookies

These cookies resemble a gingerbread cookie. It was included in my Grandmother Hodges' recipe box. This happens to be the one cookie I really cannot turn down. I make these year round because to me gingerbread is not just a Christmas Holiday Cookie. Try a drizzle of chocolate over the cookies once they are cooled. These also make an excellent ice cream sandwich cookie with coffee or vanilla ice cream.

3/4 cup Crisco

1 cup sugar

1 egg

1/4 cup molasses

1 1/2 teaspoons cinnamon

1/2 teaspoon salt

1 teaspoon ground ginger

1/2 teaspoon ground cloves

2 cups all-purpose flour

2 teaspoons baking soda

Additional granulated sugar
    for rolling cookies

1. **Preheat oven to 375 degrees.**
2. In the bowl of your hand mixture, **beat the shortening and add sugar gradually until fluffy.** This takes about 5 minutes.
3. **Add** egg and molasses and mix well.
4. In a separate bowl **combine** the spices, salt, flour, baking soda and salt. You can whisk these together.
5. **Add the dry ingredients** to the creamed mixture 1/4 cup at a time.
6. **Chill one hour** or until you can handle the dough without it feeling super sticky.
7. **Roll into 1" balls**. Roll balls in granulated sugar.
8. **Place on** ungreased baking sheet. Do not flatten.
9. **Bake for 10 minutes.** Store in airtight containers.

desserts

peanut butter balls

If I had to select one recipe that reminds me the most of my Mom's Mom, Nanny, this would be it. Making these every Christmas was, and is, a family staple. Nanny and Mom would gather together grandchildren for an afternoon of peanut butter ball making. It is such a treasured memory. The recipe doubles well and you can freeze the finished balls. They make great gifts and party desserts. You can find the Gulf Wax in the canning section of your grocery store.

2 sticks of butter, softened

1 1/2 cups graham cracker crumbs

1/2 cup crunchy peanut butter

1 box powdered sugar (1 pound)

1 cup pecans, finely chopped

1 teaspoon vanilla extract

Coating

16 ounce bag chocolate chips

1/4 block Gulf wax
   (I know, weird, but needed),
   cut into smaller pieces with a knife

1. In a medium mixing bowl, **combine** butter, graham cracker crumbs and peanut butter. **Add in** powdered sugar and combine. **Mix in** pecans and vanilla. This mixture is very thick.

2. **Roll into 1 inch balls.** The mixture will hold together well if you squeeze it in your hands a few times first and then roll the 1 inch ball.

3. In a small glass bowl or 2 cup liquid measuring cup, **add chocolate chips and small pieces of wax. Place in** the microwave for 45 seconds. **Stir. Heat** for another 45 seconds. **Stir**. If the chocolate is not melted and smooth, heat one more time for 30 seconds.

4. Using a toothpick or dipping tool, **dip each ball in the chocolate** and place on a piece of parchment or wax paper to **cool and set.**

5. You can put these in large baggies and freeze, if your family doesn't eat them all first!

nancy lou's pecan pie

Christmas and Thanksgiving always include a pecan pie and a pumpkin pie. My Mom's pecan pie is always beautiful. She takes the time to perfectly arrange the pecans in a circular pattern. Sometimes she makes a chocolate version of this pie as well. I think some years we should start with pie so that we are not so full from turkey when it becomes pie time.

3 eggs

1 cup sugar

1 cup light corn Syrup

4 tablespoons butter, melted

1 teaspoon vanilla extract

1 teaspoon white vinegar

1 cup pecans halves

1 prepared pie shell or homemade pie dough

1. **Preheat oven to 450°.**
2. **Beat eggs and sugar** until light and fluffy. This take about 5 minutes.
3. **Add** syrup, butter, extract and vinegar. **Pour the mixture** into the pie shell.
4. **Arrange the pecans** in a circular pattern.
5. **Bake for 10 minutes**. Then reduce heat to 350°. Bake for another 50 minutes. **Cool and serve.**

pumpkin pie

My Mom created all of our Thanksgiving dinners until I was 45 years old. At that point I told her it was time I learned how to roast a turkey. The pie portion of Thanksgiving dinner is still something she makes every year. Thank goodness I have her recipe. You can make your own pie dough if you would like. The pie dough recipe is with the Lemon Chiffon Pie recipe.

2 cups cooked pumpkin

    (this can be fresh or canned)

2 teaspoons melted butter

1 cup sugar

1/2 teaspoon salt

1/2 teaspoon cinnamon

1 cup milk

2 eggs, plus an egg for the egg wash

1 prepared pie shell or

    homemade pie dough

1. **Preheat oven to 450°.**
2. **Combine all ingredients**, stirring well after adding each.
3. **Brush bottom** of pie shell with egg wash to prevent a soggy crust. This is the best tip!
4. **Pour in mixture.**
5. **Bake for 10 minutes**. Reduce heat to 350 degrees and bake another 50 minutes.

oreo cookie ice cream dessert

Everyone enjoys this dessert. I have found that most people can pick a part that is their favorite. I love the Oreo crust. Others like that you can change the ice cream to other favorite flavors like chocolate chip mint or coffee ice cream. This is a great summer dessert and holds in the freezer for several weeks. I always let it sit at room temperature for about 15 minutes before serving. This makes it easier to slice.

24 Oreo Cookies, crushed

1/2 cup butter, melted

1/2 gallon vanilla ice cream
(or favorite flavor), softened

___

1/2 cup butter

2/3 cup sugar

2/3 cup evaporated milk (5 oz can)

1 teaspoon vanilla extract

1/4 teaspoon salt

1 German chocolate square

8 ounce container Cool Whip

1/2 cup chopped pecans.

1. **Crush the Oreo Cookies** in the food processor. **Sprinkle** Oreos in 9 x 13 pan.
2. **Pour 1/2 cup melted butter** over cookies.
3. **Spread softened ice cream** over crumbs and freeze.
4. While the ice cream layer is chilling **make the sauce**. In a sauce pan **combine** 1/2 cup butter, sugar, evaporated milk, vanilla and salt. **Whisk** this mixture while it comes to a boil.
5. **Add chocolate square** to dissolve in the hot mixture.. Then cool and pour over frozen ice cream.
6. **Top with Cool Whip** and sprinkle with nuts.
7. **Cover** with plastic wrap and foil, then return to the freezer.

Wrapped, this dish keeps for weeks.

Variation: After the chocolate layer, add salted peanuts. This gives you the sweet and salty combination that is perfect.

crusty pound cake

When you make this, remember the title of the recipe, "crusty"! It is just that! I've had people say I keep looking for a pan that gives me even better "crust to surface" ratio. If I could just cut off the crusty part and eat that I would every time. If this is cooked in a loaf pan, the end of the loaf is the best piece! This is one of the pound cake recipes from my Grandmother Hodges.

1 cup butter

3 cups sugar

6 eggs

3 cups all-purpose flour, whisked

2 cups whipping cream

1 teaspoon vanilla extract

desserts

1. This cake starts its baking process with **a cold oven.** No preheating needed or wanted.

2. Whenever possible, **all ingredients should be room temperature.**

3. In a stand mixer, **cream the butter and sugar** until light yellow and fluffy. This actually takes about 5 minutes.

4. **Add eggs one at a time**, beating well after each egg.

5. **Add flour and cream** alternating and ending with flour.

6. **Add vanilla extract.**

7. **Using a bundt pan or two loaf pans, butter them and then dust both with flour**. This step pays off in the end. You do not want these cakes to stick in the pan. The cook time will not change because you are using loaf pans instead of a bundt pan.

8. **Place in a cold oven. Turn on oven to 300°.** Bake for 1 hour and 25 minutes. Let cool in pans for 10 minutes. Then remove from the pan to cool.

brown sugar pound cake

My Grandfather, my Dad's Dad, was a surgeon. Many people have told me that if my grandfather told them to cut their head off and sew it on backwards they would. He gave me credit for keeping his stitching skills honed. I was always trying to keep up with my brother and his best friend which often ended in an injury requiring stitches. When he retired from his practice he began baking pound cakes. The brown sugar version was one of his most popular. I remember finding this recipe on his Commodore 64 computer! That still cracks me up.

1 stick butter

1 cup Crisco

1 cup granulated sugar

2 2/3 cups light brown sugar

1 teaspoon almond extract

1 teaspoon butter extract

5 eggs

3 cups cake flour

1/4 teaspoon salt

1/2 tablespoon baking powder

1 cup canned evaporated milk

1 1/2 cups chopped pecans
   (Optional)

1. **Preheat oven to 325 degrees.**
2. Using a stand mixer, **cream the butter and shortening** together. Gradually **add the sugars**.
3. **Add the extracts. Add the eggs one at a time.**
4. **Whisk together** the dry ingredients. **Add** dry ingredients alternatively with the evaporated milk.
5. **Dredge pecans** in flour and fold into batter. **Pour in** greased and floured Bundt pan.
6. **Bake for 1 1/2 hours** or till done. Test with tooth pick. Do not over bake. This dish will still jiggle even when it is cooked. Do not cook it until the jiggle disappears.
7. **Cool in the pan for 10 minutes.** Remove from pan and allow to cool completely.

cream cheese pound cake

A good Southern girl has multiple pound cake recipes at her finger tips.
I am trying so hard to be good. This recipe creates a pound cake with a soft
exterior and a moist interior. It is a classic dish and can be altered by adding
almond extract, chocolate chips or strawberries.

desserts

3 sticks unsalted butter,
    room temperature

3 cups sugar

6 eggs

8 ounce package cream cheese,
    room temperature

3 cups all-purpose flour, sifted 3 times

1/4 teaspoon salt

1 teaspoon vanilla extract

1. **Preheat oven to 325 degrees.**
2. **Butter a 10" loaf pan.** Cut parchment paper to fit the bottom of the loaf pan.
3. **Sprinkle sides** with a little sugar.
4. In a stand mixer bowl, **beat butter and sugar** until fluffy and smooth.
5. **Cut cream cheese** into six cubes. **Add eggs** one at a time alternating with cubed cream cheese.
6. **Add flour slowly.**
7. **Finally add** salt and vanilla. **Pour in** prepared pan.
8. **Bake for for 90 minutes.** Allow to cool in the pan for 10 minutes. Remove from the pan and allow to cool completely.

chocolate pound cake

My mother loves chocolate. Her bridge club loves chocolate. It's true, I am a big fan as well. This pound cake hits the chocolate spot. You can eat it as is or ice with a chocolate frosting or a vanilla glaze. Try toasting the second day and topping with a pat of butter. Not bad, not bad at all.

2 sticks unsalted butter

1/2 cup Crisco

3 cups sugar

5 eggs

3 cups all-purpose flour

1/2 teaspoon baking powder

1/2 teaspoon salt

5 heaping teaspoons cocoa powder

1 cup milk

1 teaspoon vanilla extract

1. **Preheat oven to 325 degrees.**
2. In a mixer bowl, **cream together** the butter, Crisco and sugar for 4 - 5 minutes.
3. **Add eggs**, one at a time.
4. In a bowl **add flour, baking powder, salt and cocoa**. Whisk together.
5. **Add** one third of the flour mixture. Then **add 1/2 of milk**. **Add** another third of the flour mixture. **Add** remaining milk. **Add** final portion of flour.
6. **Grease and flour** a bundt pan or loaf pan.
7. **Bake** on a sheet pan (just in case it spills) **for 1 hour and 30 - 45 minutes.**
8. **Cool in the pan for 10 minutes.**
9. You can use the chocolate icing recipe on this cake from the Mrs. Atlanta Chocolate Cake. It is also good as it is.

whoopie pies

Whoopie Pies became part of my life when I married Dick. He is from Lancaster, Pennsylvania, in the heart of Pennsylvania Dutch Country. They are a significant part of his life, having been served at birthday parties, picnics and after school activities. Each one is like having your own cake, but with a creamy filling instead of icing. Today we would call this a deconstructed donut! His mother shared this recipe with me. They are now part of my Christmas Cookie tray giving.

The Cake Portion

1 cup Crisco

2 cups sugar

2 eggs

4 cups all-purpose flour

1 cup cocoa

2 teaspoons salt

1 cup buttermilk

2 teaspoons baking soda

3/4 cup hot water

The Creamy Filling

2 egg whites

4 tablespoons all-purpose flour

4 tablespoons milk

2 teaspoons vanilla extract

1 1/4 cup Crisco

1 (1 pound) bag powdered sugar

1. **Preheat oven to 400 degrees.**
2. **For the cake portion**: In the bowl of a stand mixer, **cream Crisco and sugar** for about 3 minutes.
3. **Add eggs** one at a time and beat.
4. In a separate bowl **whisk together flour, cocoa and salt.**
5. **Add flour and buttermilk** to mixer, alternating and ending with flour.
6. **Dissolve baking soda** in hot water. **Add to mixture**.
7. **Drop** by small cookie scoop full onto an ungreased cookie sheet.
8. **Bake for 8 minutes.**
9. **For the filling: beat egg whites** until you form soft peaks.
10. **Fold in** flour then milk. **Add** vanilla.
11. **Beat in Crisco** and slowly **add powdered sugar**.
12. **Spread** between cooled cookies.
13. Keeps well in refrigerator and each whoopee pie can be individually wrapped and frozen.

1-2-3-4 cake

A cake recipe you can memorize is a beautiful thing! The cake bakes up similar to a pound cake. It is a great cake for sculpting and decorative icing and fondant. I like to spread my favorite jam on the layers of cake and spread the icing on the jam. It makes for a flavorful icing in-between the cake layers. The ingredients are listed below in their 1-2-3-4 order to make it easier to remember. However, the directions explain what order the ingredients should be added.

Cake

1 cup butter, room temperature

2 cups sugar

3 cups all-purpose flour

4 eggs, room temperature

3 teaspoons baking powder

1 cup buttermilk, room temperature

1 teaspoon vanilla extract

1. All ingredients need to be **room temperature**. Feel free to get them out and leave them on the counter the night before you bake.
2. **Preheat oven to 325 degrees.**
3. In a mixing bowl, **cream together** butter and sugar for 5 minutes. **Add eggs** one at a time. Please crack each egg into a bowl and then add. No one wants eggshells in their cake. **Combine well** between each egg.
4. **Add** vanilla. **Add** flour and milk. Start with flour and end with flour.
5. You may bake this in (2) 9 inch round pans, a bundt pan or a large rectangular pan.
6. **Bake for 40 - 45 minutes.** Cool for 10 minutes in the pan. Remove from pan and cool completely before icing.

Icing

1 cup sugar

2 tablespoons corn syrup

8 tablespoons water

4 egg whites

2 teaspoons vanilla or almond extract

1. Create a double boiler. **Bring water to a boil.**
2. **Add all ingredients except extract** into a medium metal bowl. **Set over** boiling water. Water should not touch the bottom of the bowl.
3. Use a hand mixer while the mixture is in the double boiler and **mix until stiff.** **Add** 1 teaspoon of vanilla and/or almond extract.
4. **Spread icing** over cake. Icing will crack as is hardens.

a Southern Legacy

crock fruit cake

There is a funny story that goes with the recreation of this recipe. All of my grandmother's recipes are in her cursive handwriting. Her handwriting is very swirly and elegant. Sometimes it is hard to interpret the letters. I love her Fruit Cake Cookies so I wanted to make her version of a fruit cake as well. The recipe card for her fruit cake looks like it says "Crack" Fruit Cake. I researched "crack Fruit" everywhere. I even asked several celebrity chefs if they have ever heard of "Crack Fruit". No one knew anything. While teaching a class for Seniors, I mentioned my quest for information about"Crack Fruit". A week later I received an email from one of the Seniors. She went to Tennessee and mentioned what I was looking for to a Tennessee native. This person told her that it was probably Crock Fruit. Low and behold I found a Brandied Fruit Recipe in the files. The Brandied Fruit is also known as Crock Fruit. Mystery solved and the cake has been recreated!

1 1/4 cups canola oil

1 1/2 cups sugar

3 eggs, well beaten

2 teaspoons vanilla extract

1 teaspoon baking soda

1 teaspoon salt

2 cups all-purpose flour

3 cups Crock Fruit, drained, see recipe

1 cup chopped pecans

Icing

1/2 cup butter

1 cup brown sugar

1/4 cup evaporated milk

1 teaspoon vanilla extract

1. **Preheat the oven to 325 degrees. Butter and flour a loaf or bundt pan.**
2. In the bowl of your stand mixer, **cream the oil and sugar** for 4 minutes.
3. **Add the eggs and vanilla** and beat until the mixture is fluffy.
4. In a separate bowl, **whisk together the dry ingredients**. Add the pecans.
5. Beat in the dry ingredients with the butter mixture.
6. **Fold in** the crock fruit. **Pour into** the prepared loaf pan.
7. **Bake for 1 hour and 15 minutes.** Cool in the pan for 10 minutes. Remove from the pan.
8. In a sauce plan, **melt the butter. Add the brown sugar and evaporated milk**. Bring the ingredients to a boil. **Remove from the heat. Add the vanilla extrac**t. Pour over the warm cake.

brandied fruit
aka crock fruit

This recipe requires patience and a little bit of love. My Grandmother Hodges made this recipe for a cake and she served this "happy" fruit over ice cream. It is important to cover this while it is fermenting but do not seal it tightly. The lid will pop right off if it doesn't get air! Canned fruit works better than fresh fruit.

1st week – 1 large can sliced peaches drained, 1 cup sugar, 1 cup brandy, stir every day or so

2nd week – Drain the fruit and add 1 large can pineapple chunks drained, 1 cup sugar, stir every day or so

3rd week – Drain the fruit and add 1 cup sugar, 2 cans queen anne cherries (pitted), stir every day or so

4th week – Drain the fruit and add 1 cup sugar, 2 cans peeled apricots (pitted), stir every day or so

Once you have gone through the process, you can store the fruit in an airtight container in the refrigerator.

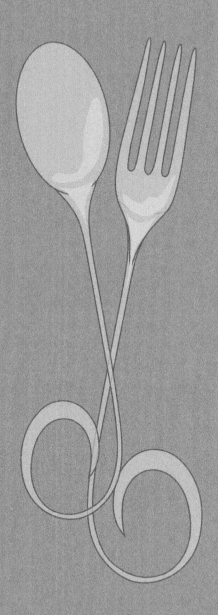

bless your heart

boiled peanuts

My stepfather, Watson, ate peanuts all the time; football games, road trips, baseball games, picnics or watching a good movie. In his 90's, there were always peanut shells around his chair. I still have one of his peanut buckets. He is the one who introduced me to boiled peanuts. I didn't initially fall in love. It was an acquired taste. Now, I will drive many miles to get the hot, salted juicy, perfect boiled peanut. I am grateful that it is easy to find raw peanuts in the grocery store these days. I perfected my boiled peanut making one summer when Mom and Watson had a beach house in Port St. Joe, Florida. I believe I kept a pot of boiled peanuts in the works every time we visited. These are best served in a large styrofoam cup with a brown bag for the shells.

*Variations: Add 1/2 chopped garlic
when boiling for
Garlic Boiled Peanuts.
Add a 1/2 cup Cajun Seasoning to
the soaking stage. Then add Crab
Boil to the boiling portion for
Cajun Boiled Peanuts.*

2 pounds Raw or Green peanuts

1 1/2 cups salt

3 gallons of water

1. If you are using raw peanuts, **place them in a large pot. Add 1/2 cup of salt and cover with water.** Let this sit for 8 hours. **Drain and rinse** the peanuts. If you are using Green Peanuts you can skip this step.

2. **Add 3 gallons of water** to the peanuts and **1 cup of salt.**

3. **Bring to a boil** over high heat. Lower to medium heat and **cook for 3 hours.** If using green peanuts this cooking time will only be about 1 hour. At this point, **check your peanuts. You do not want a crunchy peanut.** It should have a soft texture but maintain the look of a peanut. **Cook in 30 minute increments** as needed to get the peanuts to the desired texture.

4. **Allow the peanuts to cool in the water for at least 30 minutes.**

5. Boiled peanuts will keep in the refrigerator for 1 week.

spicy cornbread

My Mom loved to make all kinds of bread. Having a bread dish at every evening meal was something Watson, my stepfather, expected. Typically we had regular cornbread or biscuits. Sometimes it was something as simple as a piece of sliced bread. Many times my Mom would surprise us with new recipes she found in the newspaper or a magazine. I would call this recipe her "fancy" version of cornbread. I've made it for all types of celebrations, even non-cornbread eaters seem to enjoy this version. I have a client that requests this every week. Now that's real love!

1 cup self-rising cornmeal

1/2 teaspoon baking soda

1/4 teaspoon salt

1 1/2 cups cheddar cheese

1/2 cup chopped onion

1 cup milk

3 teaspoons bacon drippings

1 teaspoon garlic powder

3 eggs, beaten

7 oz whole kernel corn, drained

3 jalapeños, chopped

1. **Preheat oven to 350 degrees. Place cast iron pan into the oven to heat.**
2. **Combine first three ingredients** in a medium bowl. Whisk them to combine.
3. Create a well in the dried ingredients. **Add the remaining ingredients and stir to combine them.**
4. **Pour into greased and heated cast iron skillet** or baking pan.
5. **Bake for 45 minutes.** Let cool in the pan for 15 minutes.
6. **Serve hot** with lots of salted butter.

a Southern Legacy

chili con queso

My Aunt Sue makes a killer Mexican buffet dinner. She would slow roast pork butt in smokey and spicy seasonings. For a great topping buffet, chop all the toppings you could ever hope for on a taco or burrito. Then this slightly spicy and very cheesy dish would be added. There was always so much yummy food. It spoiled me to any restaurant version of tacos. This recipe is a must when you create your next Mexican dinner. Combine it with John's Guacamole and the Strawberry Salsa with chips. I served it to 200 employees and baseball coaches when I worked for the Parks department. It is an evening they still talk about. They loved the cheesy, spicy goodness!

7 ounce jar whole green chiles

2 cups monterey jack cheese, grated

2 cups cheddar cheese, grated

1/4 cup salsa

3 eggs

1/4 cup all-purpose flour

1/2 cup heavy cream

1. Preheat oven to 250 degrees.
2. Spray 9 x 13 casserole pan.
3. Combine cheeses. Layer cheese, chiles, cheese, chiles, etc. until you run out. Cheese should end on top.
4. Pour salsa over mixture.
5. Blend eggs, flour and cream. Pour over casserole. This should come to the top of the casserole pan.
6. Bake at 250° until fluffy, about 25 minutes.

aunt sue's hushpuppies

In the 80's and 90's my Aunt Sue was famous for her "fish fry" evenings. All of the family was invited for this feast. Several times she even created it on vacation. They included fried catfish and shrimp, a tangy coleslaw and these hushpuppies. I have a host of really good hushpuppy recipes, but this one is my favorite. The beer you select can change the flavor. With an IPA beer, the flavor is subtle and the beer gives lightness to the hushpuppies. As you move to a darker beer, the more beer flavor you get. If you are cooking for someone with a nut allergy, you can fry in a vegetable oil.

1 cup cornmeal mix

1 cup self-rising flour

1/2 cup finely chopped onions

1 egg, beaten

1 cup of beer, you choose

Peanut Oil

1. **Combine cornmeal, flour and onions** in a medium bowl.

2. **Add the beer** until the mix is wet. It should look like cornbread batter. As a toast to your meal drink whatever beer you have left!

3. **Add the egg** and mix into the batter. Let stand for 15 - 30 minutes. Batter should now be thick.

4. In a Dutch Oven or a large deep pan **heat about 2 inches of oil** to 360 degrees.

5. **Drop the batter by teaspoons** full into the hot oil. I use a small ice cream scoop. **Cook** until the first side in the oil is a golden brown. **Flip and cook the other side** to the same color.

6. **Place on paper towels** or on newspaper to drain. Sprinkle with salt.

moo burger

When my Mom and Dad married, they were living in Nashville. Tennessee. My Dad was attending Vanderbilt University. During Dad's freshman year, my older brother, John, was born. Mom was always trying to make yummy meals on a budget, and Moo Burgers became a great answer to her dinner question. They are good cooked in the oven, on the stove top or on the grill.

1 1/2 pounds ground beef

1 cup sour cream

1/4 cup Worcestershire sauce

1 tablespoon onion flakes

1 1/2 teaspoons salt

1 1/2 cups corn flakes, lightly crushed

1. **Combine all ingredients in a bowl**. You want to mix the ingredients together without over working your beef.

2. **Shape into 8 patties** about 3/4 inch thick. Place on a rack on a sheet pan to **broil or grill for 5 minutes on the first side and 2 1/2 minutes on second side.**

3. You can eat these alone or turn them into a true burger with all the toppings.

a Southern Legacy

bless

strawberry salsa

This recipe became a part of my life in my early 20's when I took it to many parties. I truly can not remember how or where I found the original. I know I have tweaked it over the years to what it is today. I promise this is a wonderful and an unexpected taste. Pair this with John's Guacamole and chips. Try this on grilled pork, fish or chicken. You could even mix in cooked shrimp and serve on a buffet. Dick, my husband, loves this salsa!

6 tablespoons olive oil
2 tablespoons white balsamic vinegar
1/2 teaspoon salt
1 pint strawberries, coarsely chopped
8 green onions, chopped
2 pints grape or cherry tomatoes, halved
1/2 cup chopped fresh cilantro

1. **Whisk together first three** ingredients to emulsify the dressing.
2. **Gently stir** in the remaining ingredients.
3. **Chill one hour**.
4. **Serve** with tortilla chips or corn chips.

john's guacamole

I believe guacamole recipes are as personal as mac-n-cheese and chicken salad recipes. My brother John created this version over 25 years ago. John made the best breakfasts, Bloody Marys and guacamole. He was a Navy man and spent time in San Antonio, Texas. I believe it was then that he perfected this recipe. You can make it smooth or chunky, but no matter how you make it, it will not last long with a bowl of tortilla chips and salsa nearby.

5 ripe avocados

3 Roma tomatoes, seeded

5 green onions

1/4 cup Hellman's Mayonaisse

1/4 cup sour cream

salt/pepper to taste

juice of one lime

2 tablespoons white vinegar
　　or apple cider vinegar

1. For **smooth guacamole**, **process all ingredients** in a food processor.
2. For a **chunky version**, **mash the avocados** with a fork. Then **finely dice** your tomatoes and green onions. **Stir into** the avocados. **Add remaining** ingredients and stir to combine.
3. To store, place plastic wrap directly on the guacamole to help prevent discoloration.

bless

nutty fingers

What cookie makes you think of your teenage years? For me this recipe is it hands down. My Mom made these at the holidays, of course. I also remember them at many other gatherings or every day occurrences. When you store them in an airtight container they keep very well. Combine with the Peanut Butter Balls and Pound Cake Cookies on a tray and you have a great dessert combination.

---

1 1/4 sticks butter

1 tablespoon ice water

1 teaspoon vanilla extract

4 tablespoons powdered sugar

1 cup pecans or walnuts, chopped

2 cups all-purpose flour

1. **Preheat oven to 350 degrees.**
2. In a mixer bowl, **cream butter and sugar** for 3 minutes.
3. **Add** vanilla, water, and flour, then nuts. **Mix** until combined.
4. **Pinch off small pieces** and shape in the palm of your hand as a crescent moon shape.
5. **Bake for 20 minutes.** Cool slightly. **Roll in powdered sugar.**

bless

a Southern Legacy

walnut date bars

I worked for Cobb County, Georgia Parks Department in the Arts section for 29 years. Part of my job included participating in our State Wide Parks and Arts Organizations. This meant periodic road trips. Two of my coworkers traveled with me more than any others: Nelah Gabler and Eddie Canon. They loved these snack bars. Nelah would always be disappointed on a car trip if these were not included. They are easy to make, store well and two people I really care about enjoy them. Perfection!

---

1 package yellow cake mix

3/4 cup packed brown sugar

3/4 cup melted butter

2 eggs

2 cups chopped dates

2 cups chopped walnuts

1 cup dried cranberries

1. **Preheat oven to 350 degrees.** Grease a 9 x 13 pan.
2. In a large bowl for your mixer, **combine cake mix and brown sugar.**
3. **Add melted butter and eggs.** Beat 2 minutes at medium speed.
4. In another bowl **combine dates, walnuts and cranberries.** Stir.
5. **Add date mixture to the cake mixture.** Stir until well blended.
6. **Spread into greased pan.**
7. **Bake** until edges are golden brown, **30 - 45 minutes.** Cool for 10 minutes in the pan. Run a knife around edges to loosen contents. Then cool for one hour before cutting into squares. Store in an air tight container.

a Southern Legacy

honey french dressing

I do not see French dressing very often any more. I remember a very orange version at restaurants and in bottles while I was growing up. My Grandmother Hodges had very few dressings in her recipe box and I am very happy that this version of a dressing is among them. I encourage you to try this tart and sweet dressing! Salad should never be boring in flavor or color. This dressing has a great red-orange color and never disappoints your tastes buds.

1 1/4 cups Canola oil

1/2 teaspoon salt

1 tablespoon Worcestershire sauce

1/3 cup chili sauce

3/4 cup apple cider vinegar

1 small onion, grated

1/3 cup honey

1. **Mix all ingredients** in a medium bowl. I do not make this one in the food processor or with an immersion blender. I like to keep the texture by whisking it by hand.
2. **Keep in air tight jar** in the refrigerator. **Shake well** before using.
3. Keeps for 3-4 weeks. Makes 3 cups.

homemade ranch dressing

Ranch dressing in an old mayonnaise jar was always in our refrigerator when I was growing up. It was made with mayonaisse, buttermilk and a packet of seasonings. It was almost everyone's dressing of choice and I suspect, for my Mom, it was easy to make and to keep on hand when feeding several people. I will say that the dry seasoning mixed used can be helpful but I knew that it could be recreated and take Ranch dressing to another level! I came up with this version for children to make in small batches in baby food jars. It always ends with the "shake it, shake it" dance. That's the best part of making this dressing. Don't forget the fun!

1/2 cup Hellman's Mayonaisse

2 tablespoons buttermilk (more if you need it for consistency)

1 teaspoon Worcestershire sauce

1/2 teaspoon salt

1/4 teaspoon black pepper

Dash of hot sauce

2 garlic cloves, grated

1/4 red onion, grated

1 tablespoon each chopped chives, parsley, basil, tarragon and dill

   (throw in oregano, cilantro or mint if desired)

1 teaspoon apple cider vinegar

   (I have also used various flavored vinegars)

1. **Place all ingredients in a mason jar or old mayonnaise jar.**
2. Do the **"shake it, shake it"** dance to combine.
3. You can also put everything in a blender or food processor and combine that way.
4. Kids LOVE to make this recipe and do the dance. Enjoy!

a Southern Legacy

greek olive tapenade

Did you know that a rosemary plant will grow to fit the container it is in? How do I know this? I purchased a 12" tall plant several years ago. We decided to move the plant from its planter in front of the house to a raised garden bed in the backyard. Skip forward a couple of years and pow I now have a rosemary tree that I can decorate for Christmas. With this rosemary tree, I need to use rosemary as often as possible. I discovered this delicious tapenade decades ago. With the rosemary required, we use this recipe more often. It works well as a dip or a spread, but you can also stuff chicken or pork with it before baking to create a Greek dish. However, some days you only need a spoon, the tapenade and some crackers.

1 cup Kalamata olives, pitted

1 tablespoon fresh rosemary, pulled from the stem

1 garlic clove

1/2 teaspoon salt

Juice of one lime

1/2 cup Parmesan cheese

1/2 cup pecans, walnuts or pine nuts

1/2 cup olive oil or avocado oil

1. **Combine all ingredients except** the olive oil in the food processor.

2. **Stream in olive oil** as you process the ingredients. You want a coarse, moist mixture.

3. **Serve on endive or crackers.**

bless

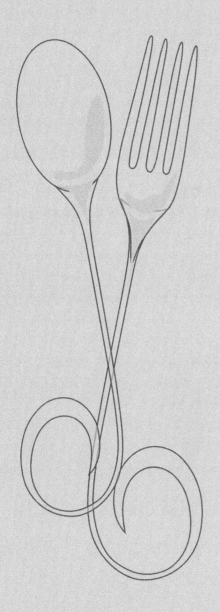

when life gives you
lemons

lemon fluff

I love the name of this recipe. My Grandmother Hodges gave all of her grandchildren a box of her hand written recipes. The name of this dessert makes me giggle; it has since the first day I read this recipe in my box. Just saying "Lemon Fluff" makes me smile. It evokes memories of the gracious entertaining world of the 1960's and 1970's. Lemon Fluff pulls together easily accessible ingredients and creates an excellent dessert. I love the tips at the end of the recipe. This recipe also teaches you how to make a lemon curd. Lemon curd can be used to fill small tarts, as an icing for pound cake or as a topping on ice cream. My grandmother loved lemon desserts because they are generally light and refreshing.

1 package unflavored gelatin

1/3 cup cold water

1 Angel Food Cake (store bought is fine)

6 egg yolks

1 teaspoon lemon zest

1 1/2 cups sugar, divided

3/4 cup lemon juice

6 egg whites

1 cup whipping cream

1/3 cup sugar

Food coloring, optional

1. **Dissolve** gelatin in the cold water.

2. To make the lemon custard or lemon curd, **create a double boiler**. This is a sauce pan with about an inch of water and a heat resistant bowl on top. In the bowl of a double boiler, **add egg yolks, lemon zest, 3/4 cup sugar and lemon juice**. Over medium heat whisk until thickened. Add gelatin to cooked hot mixture. Do not let it congeal yet. Remove from the heat and stir occasionally. You need to slightly cool the custard before adding this mixture to the others.

3. In a bowl, **shred angel food cake** into small pieces.

4. In another bowl, **beat egg whites and 1/3 cup sugar** until stiff (adding sugar a little bit at a time).

5. **Fold together lemon custard, egg white and shredded cake**. Place in a lightly greased bundt pan. Let stand overnight in refrigerator.

6. Just before serving, **beat whipping cream and 1/3 cup sugar** until stiff, but still shiny.

7. **To serve**, run knife around edge of pan. Un-mold onto silver tray or plate. Ice with whipped cream.

Color whipped cream, yellow, pink or green - your choice.
Decorate with fresh flowers, fruit or homemade lemon cookies.
Beautiful ending to a meal!

honey butter chicken

This is it!! The recipe I make as often as possible. It is always my daughter, Caroline's, first request! This recipe caught my attention immediately when I started reading Kathleen Howard Rambo's cookbook. She was so brave as to tell me right up front that a main ingredient to this dish is butter. What you don't realize until reading the ingredients list is that you have lemon and honey as well! So yummy! I've served this for dinner parties, buffet lines and even appetizers. The recipe works with whole breasts, chicken tenderloins and even bite sized pieces. Thank you Kathleen Howard Rambo for another winning recipe!

3 pounds boneless, skinless chicken breast halves

1/2 cup butter, melted

1 cup all-purpose flour

Sauce:

1/4 cup butter, melted

1 teaspoon paprika

1/2 teaspoon salt

1/4 teaspoon pepper

1/2 cup honey

1/4 cup lemon juice

1. **Preheat oven to 400 degrees.**
2. **Prepare chicken**; trim as needed, cube it or make strips depending on how you plan to serve this dish. Small breast halves work well when serving chicken whole.
3. **Place butter** in a 9 x 13 baking pan. Melt in the oven.
4. **Mix flour, paprika, salt and pepper** together in a shallow bowl.
5. **Roll chicken in mixture** and place onto the butter in pan. Cover and bake at 400 degrees for 30 minutes.
6. **Meanwhile: mix butter, honey and lemon juice together.** After chicken has baked for 30 minutes, remove it from the oven. Turn the chicken over, pour sauce over chicken and return it to the oven uncovered for 25 to 35 more minutes or until the meat thermometer has reached 160 degrees.

I like to serve with my Rice and Mushroom dish and a salad.

lemons

lemon garlic dressing

I fell in love with a heavenly garlic and lemon dressing while working for the Cultural Affairs Division of the Cobb County Parks Department for our county. My Parks family loved to cook and eat together. We cooked for department meetings, softball tournaments, theatre productions and so many other events. Having a salad on a hot day and then adding a super lemony dressing was a highlight of many meals. A coworker named Donna started my love for garlic lemon dressing. Well done Donna!!

12 garlic cloves

3/4 cup olive oil (not extra virgin, too strong)

3/4 cup fresh lemon juice (fresh is important)

1/4 cup red wine vinegar

1 tablespoon Splenda or sugar (Splenda and sugar are exchanged in equal amounts)

1 teaspoon salt

1 tablespoon Dijon mustard

1. **Place all ingredients** in a food processor, blender or cup for use with an immersion blender.
2. **Blend and store.**
3. This dressing stores for 2- 3 weeks in the refrigerator.

lemons

frozen lemon bisque

I truly enjoy a good bisque. A creamy, light, highly seasoned soup tastes so good to me. You can serve a fruit, seafood or vegetable version and I am super happy. I had expected this recipe to create a soup, but it turns out this is more of a airy frozen lemon custard. I wish I could ask my Grandmother Hodges why she used the word "bisque" in the title. It is a wonderfully light and very creamy lemony ending to a meal. I guess by definition it is a frozen bisque!

4 eggs, separated

1 cup sugar, divided

Juice of 4 to 5 lemons

1 teaspoon lemon zest

1 1/4 cup evaporated milk, chilled

Graham cracker crumbs

Yellow food coloring, optional

whipping cream, optional

mint leaves, optional

1. **Chill** a metal bowl and chill the evaporated milk.
2. **Create a double boiler:** use a large sauce pan. Add about an inch of water to the pan. Bring to a soft boil. Add a metal bowl onto of the top of the sauce pan. Make sure the water doesn't touch the bottom of the bowl. In the bowl of the double boiler **whisk egg yolks, 1/2 cup sugar, lemon juice and lemon zest.** Whisk until this mixture thickens.
3. **Remove the bowl** from the double boiler and allow the lemon mixture to cool.
4. With a hand mixer, **whip the egg whites** until they begin to stiffen. **Add the other 1/2 cup sugar** and beat until the egg whites are shiny and stiff.
5. Use the chilled bowl to **beat the chilled evaporated milk** until it is stiff. Be patient. This takes 10 - 15 minutes.
6. **Fold into the cooled lemon mixture.**
7. Use this mixture and **fold it into the lemon mixture**. If you want to intensify the yellow color add a drop of yellow food coloring.
8. **Butter a 9 x 13 casserole dish** and spread crushed graham crackers over the bottom of the dish. **Fill** with the custard mixture. **Top** with a sprinkling of graham crackers crumbs. **Cover** with plastic wrap and foil to protect from any freezer burn.
9. **Freeze** until set. **Cut** into squares for serving and top with a dollop of whipped cream and mint leaf.

My Mother loves to relate this mystery: she prepared these bars often when I was a child and would freeze them for bake sales or parties. However, there would never be as many in the freezer as she placed there. That's because my older brother, John, and I would eat them frozen! So yes, these do freeze well, and they are delicious cold—very cold.

1 cup butter, softened

1 cup powdered sugar

2 cups all-purpose flour

4 eggs, beaten

2 cups sugar

1 teaspoon baking powder

4 tablespoons flour

6 tablespoons lemon juice

Powdered sugar for dusting

1. **Preheat oven to 300 degrees.**
2. **To create the crust: cream together** butter, powdered sugar and flour. Spread in a greased 9 x 13 pan. Bake for 25 minutes.
3. While the crust is cooking, **whisk together eggs, sugar, baking powder, flour and lemon juice.** Pour over hot crust. Bake for 30 – 35 minutes in a 300 degree oven. Cool in the pan.
4. **Dust** with powdered sugar and cut into 2" squares.

Lemons

marinated shrimp & artichokes

My Mom and my Grandmother Hodges (my Dad's Mom) were great hostesses because they understood the importance of a lovely meal with the right group of friends, as well as taking the time to prepare their homes for company. Whether they were getting ready for bridge or an elegant evening, they prepared and worked on every detail. The fine china was used, the silver was polished and linen napkins were pressed. Everything had its perfect place. I know how to set a proper table because of these two Southern ladies. This recipe appeared in both of their recipe boxes which told me I had to try it and add it to my own recipe box. I love how simply the marinated shrimp recipe comes together and creates a "wow" factor for a party. It is also great for a buffet when entertaining. You should make it ahead of time so it will be perfect the day of the event.

1 cup vegetable oil

2 lemons, zest and juice

1/2 cup dry white wine

1 tablespoon chopped parsley

1 teaspoon sugar

1 teaspoon salt

1/4 teaspoon whole black peppercorns

1 bay leaf

1/2 teaspoon paprika

1 garlic clove, minced

2 cans artichoke hearts, drained and quartered

(1) 8 oz can sliced water chestnuts, drained

1 small red onion, thinly sliced

2 pounds medium peeled, cooked shrimp

1. **Whisk together first 10 ingredients** in a medium bowl, vegetable oil through garlic to make the marinade.

2. **In a large plastic bag, place shrimp, artichokes, onion and chestnuts.**

3. **Pour marinade over ingredients.** Place in the refrigerator for 12 - 24 hours. Serve with bread for sopping the sauce.

a Southern Legacy

lemon chiffon pie

I really enjoy a lemon pie or a coconut pie, The height of the pie, the light texture and the solid flavor win me over every time. The word "chiffon" is so perfect when describing the texture of this pie. It is airy, creamy, tart and the crust adds the crunch that brings everything together. I recommend making the pie the day before you are going to serve it to your guests. It should be refrigerated. Waiting gives the flavors time to marry and sets the pie up beautifully for slicing.

Pie Dough

1 cup all-purpose flour

7 tablespoons cold butter, cubed

1 egg yolk (you can add egg white remaining into the filling recipe)

Pinch of Salt

4 – 6 tablespoons of ice cold water

Pie Filling

1 1/2 teaspoons unflavored gelatin

1/4 cup cold water

3 eggs, separated

1 cup sugar

1/4 teaspoon salt

1/2 cup fresh lemon juice

1/2 teaspoon lemon zest

1 cup whipping cream

Lemon slices for garnishing

1. **For the Pie Dough:** Make sure all items are measured and waiting to be used before starting.
2. **In a food processor, add flour and salt.** Pulse 3 – 4 times. Add the egg yolk. Pulse another 4 times.
3. **Place cold cubed butter** in food processor. Pulse 6 times.
4. **Start processor.** And add 3 tablespoons of ice water. DO NOT add all the ice water at once. After the first 3 tablespoons are added you will add 1/2 a tablespoon at a time until the dough starts to form a ball. Too much water and a ball will never form. You will use a different amount of water every time depending on the weather. This sounds odd but it is true. If it is warm and humid you will need less liquid. During colder weather you may need all of the liquid.
5. **Place dough ball on plastic wrap.** Press into a disk and wrap. Place the dough disk in refrigerator for at least 30 minutes. You can freeze pie dough. Double wrap in plastic wrap and date and label. Keep in the freezer for up to 6 months.
6. **Preheat oven to 350 degrees.**
7. **Roll pie dough** on a well floured surface until it resembles a circle that is 2 inches larger than your pie plate. Gently roll onto your rolling pin. Transfer to pie dish and unroll. Do not push or stretch the dough into place. Instead let it "fall" into place naturally. When you stretch the dough it will try to shrink back when baking. Use a fork to prick the bottom on the pie dough (this helps to prevent a big bubble from forming during baking). If it is a warm day, I might place the dough in the pie pan in the freezer for 30 minutes. This helps to solidify the butter.

8. **Line pie dough with parchment paper** and add rice, beans or pie weights to hold down the parchment paper.
9. **Bake for 20 – 25 minutes.** Let cool with the parchment paper and pie weights on the crust.
10. **For Filling:** Prepare a double boiler. **In a medium metal bowl, add water and sprinkle gelatin into the water to proof. Add egg yolks, 1/3 cup of sugar, lemon juice and zest.** Cook over hot water whisking until it thickens. Cool but do not let it congeal.
11. With a hand mixer in a medium bowl, **beat egg whites until stiff.** Beat in salt and 1/3 cup sugar.
12. **Fold egg white mixture into the lemon mixture.** Be gentle. You do not want to kill all of those wonderful air bubbles created in your egg white mixture.
13. **Pour into cooled, pre-baked pie shell.**
14. **Pour whipping cream** into a mixing bowl. Add 1/3 cup sugar. Beat cream and sugar until it is shiny and stiff. Spread gently on lemon mixture. Place pie in the refrigerator to cool completely and set up. Garnish with twisted lemon slices.

lemon sponge custard

My Mother really enjoys the taste of lemon. Because of this fact I thought this recipe might be hers. It turns out this is another recipe from my Grandmother Hodges. She had an arsenal of lemon desserts. With the unique texture of a crazy-light sponge cake, a sponge custard is truly refreshing. I love that everyone gets their own ramekin for dessert. This makes portion control and presentation so nice. You could change this to an orange, grapefruit or mango dessert by exchanging the lemon juice for one of these other flavors. I really like having recipes that are easily changeable in flavor.

2 teaspoons butter

2 eggs, separated

2 tablespoons lemon juice

1 cup milk

2/3 cup sugar

1 teaspoon lemon zest

2 tablespoons all-purpose flour

1 cup whipping cream

1/2 cup powdered sugar

1. **Preheat** your oven to 350 degrees.
2. In a stand mixer, **cream the butter and the sugar** for 3 – 5 minutes.
3. **Add egg yolks, lemon juice and zest** to the mixing bowl. Beat until well combined. Remove the bowl from the mixer stand.
4. **Fold in flour and milk,** alternating as you add these ingredients.
5. In a medium bowl, **beat egg whites** until stiff peaks form. Fold into the lemon mixture.
6. **Place in ramekins.** Put ramekins in hot water bath. To create a water bath, place the ramekins in a casserole dish. Fill the dish with water until the water is about half way up the edge of the dishes.
7. **Bake for 30 – 35 minutes.**
8. In a medium mixing bowl, **whip the cream with the powdered sugar.** The whipped cream should be thick and shiny. If you go too far you can create sweetened butter.
9. **Serve** with sweetened whipped cream and sprinkle with lemon zest.

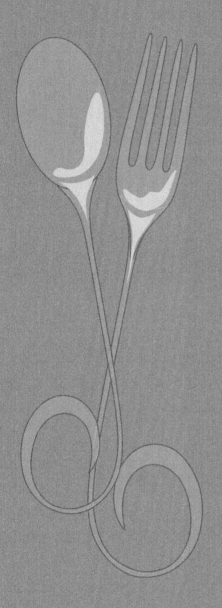

recipes for a crowd

ever crisp green tomato pickles

Nanny made tomato and watermelon rind pickles in the Spring and early Summer.
She had a big crock that lived in her laundry room during the pickling process.
We lost this crock in my Aunt Sue's house fire. I use a large Tupperware container since
I don't have a crock. In the Fall she made cucumber pickles. Everything was based on
what was in season. The flavor of these pickles is sweet, tart and has a super crunch.
Why not try them on a BBQ pork sandwich or next to your tomato, mayonnaise and
white bread sandwich?

2 cups lime powder

2 gallons water

7 pounds green tomatoes, sliced

---

2 cups white vinegar

5 pounds sugar

1 teaspoon salt

4 tablespoons pickling spice

1. **Mix together lime and water** in a very large non-metal container.
2. **Slice** the tomatoes. **Place** in lime water for 24 hours. **Rinse** them well and then **soak** in clear water for 3 hours.
3. **Drain** the tomatoes.
4. **Mix together remaining ingredients.** In a crock or large bowl **add tomatoes and cover** with vinegar mixture. Let this sit for 8 – 10 hours.
5. **Place in mason jars** for canning. Boil for 35 minutes.

party mints

I was told I would have to sell you on making these mints. So here goes: they are delicious, pretty, fun to make and something that others are not doing. These mints are soft and a nice ending to an evening meal. They can be any color or shape you wish. You could even change the flavoring to lemon or wintergreen. These mints are extra special to me because I made them for my wedding reception when I married Dick Weaver!

---

8 ounces cream cheese, softened

2 pounds powdered sugar

1 tablespoon peppermint extract

Gel food coloring of choice

Granulated sugar, for rolling

1. In a stand mixer, **beat cream cheese** until light and fluffy. Add sugar gradually and beat for 3 – 6 minutes until smooth. Add the extract.

2. **Divide** as required for various colored mints. **Add gel food coloring** and mix until color is even.

3. I use candy mold trays to create my mint shapes. **Roll mixture into small balls** that will fill each mold space. Roll each ball in granulated sugar. **Press** into the mold space. **Unmold** immediately.

4. **Place on wax paper.** Let them air dry about 45 minutes on each side. You want them to dry on both sides, so turn them over. These freeze well for the future.

This is a little time consuming but so worth it in the end.

a Southern Legacy

macaroni salad

When I married Dick Weaver, I asked his mother to send me three recipes that would make him think of home. Charmane, my mother-in-law, sent pickled beets and eggs, whoopee pies, the Pennsylvania Dutch version of chicken pot pie and macaroni salad. This recipe makes a ton of salad. The amazing thing is that if I make the whole recipe Dick Weaver will work very hard to eat it all and not share any! However, I encourage the average family to cut this recipe in half— unless you are taking it to feed a crowd.

---

1 pound elbow macaroni, cooked

2 onions, diced

2 stalks celery, diced

5 hard boiled eggs, roughly chopped

1 red, yellow or orange pepper, diced

1/2 cup sugar

3 1/2 tablespoons yellow mustard

2 1/2 cup mayonaisse

1 cup milk

1/4 cup apple cider vinegar

1/4 teaspoon salt

1. **Cook elbow macaroni** per the instructions on the box. **Drain and rinse** with cold water. This stops the cooking process. The water helps to keep the pasta from clumping while you are waiting to combine the ingredients. Set aside.

2. In a large bowl **stir together the onions, celery, eggs and red pepper.**

3. In a smaller bowl **whisk together the sugar, mustard, mayonaisse, milk, vinegar and salt.**

4. **Add macaroni** to the mayonaisse mixture. **Stir in** vegetable mixture.

5. This is best made the day before you need it. The macaroni will absorb some of the liquid. And if you aren't serving a very large crowd, just cut everything in half and then make this recipe.

Add chopped fresh broccoli or cauliflower. This would never happen to my husband's version, but I know others would enjoy!

a Southern Legacy

crowd

simple sesame cookies

I love this cookie! Why? It tastes like a sugar cookie with a surprise sesame seed taste and crunch. I happen to be a fan of simple and not overly sweet cookies. The almonds and sesame seeds give a nice crunch to these cookies. I think the flavors make for a good palate cleanser at the end of a heavy meal. For dessert, serve along side of a great sorbet or homemade ice cream. The cookies keep for several weeks in an airtight container.

2 cups butter, softened

1 1/2 cups sugar

3 cups all-purpose flour

1 cup sesame seeds

1/2 cup chopped almonds

2 cups shredded coconut

1. **Place almonds and coconut** in a food processor. Pulse 5 – 7 times. Set aside until needed.
2. In a mixing bowl: **cream together butter and sugar** until fluffy.
3. **Mix in** flour, then sesame seeds and finally the almond/coconut mixture.
4. **Divide** mixture in half. **Create** two "logs". **Wrap and roll** each log with wax or parchment paper. **Chill** for at least an hour. You can also freeze this dough.
5. **Preheat oven to 300 degrees.** When ready to bake, **slice** into 1/4" cookies. **Bake** on an ungreased or parchment paper lined cookie sheet for 20 - 25 minutes.

my go to marinara

6 cups chopped onion
   (3 medium onions)

1 tablespoon extra virgin olive oil

1 tablespoon sugar

1/2 cup dry red wine (really any wine
   works, red is my preference)

1 tablespoon extra virgin olive oil

2 teaspoons dried oregano

1 teaspoon salt

1/2 teaspoon dried thyme

1/2 teaspoon marjoram

1/2 teaspoon basil

1/2 teaspoon black pepper

1/4 teaspoon red pepper flakes

6 garlic cloves, minced

2 bay leaves

2 - 28 ounce cans crushed tomatoes

14.5 ounce can diced tomatoes

2 - 6 ounce cans tomato paste

2 cups vegetable, mushroom, chicken or
   beef stock (you can use water
   but why not add liquid AND flavor)

My introduction to marinara that didn't come from a jar happened with Mrs. Bea Ardito, my ex-husband's grandmother. "Granny", as she was known to the family, was about 4 foot 9 inches on a good day. She wore her hair in curler most of the time and always wore a moo-moo. She would start marinara in the morning. It took 6 or more hours for her sauce to finish. Her Italian food was amazing. This is not one of her sauces, but I developed it because of the layering of herbs that I learned from her. It is flavorful, freezes beautifully and is actually low calorie. What a win-win! It is good as a pasta sauce, as your sauce for lasagna and any other red sauce idea you have. This recipe makes 12 cups of marinara. You can cut this recipe in half with no issues.

---

1. In a large heated sauce pot (large enough for 12 cups of marinara) over medium high heat, **add 1 tablespoon of olive oil, onions and 1 tablespoon of sugar**. **Cook** until the onions are soft and slightly caramelized.

2. **Reduce heat** to medium. **Add red wine and reduce** the wine with the onions by half.

3. **Add another tablespoon of oil, followed by all of the herbs and spices**. Let cook for 5 minutes to allow herbs and spices to release their flavors.

4. **Add the cans** of crushed and diced tomatoes, tomato paste and choice of liquid. Now let this **simmer, covered, for 3 hours** on your stove top over medium low heat. **Stir every now and then.** No one wants to clean burned-on tomato sauce off a pan!

This freezes very well. You can use it as a pasta sauce, in lasagna, as a pizza sauce and even as dip for crusty bread.

tea cakes

This recipe is from my Grandmother Hodges' collection. When you think of serving tea, these cookies are a perfect addition. They are not terribly sweet. They are actually lovely served with whipped cream and jam, like a scone. I am bringing it back because the ingredient list includes a "wine glass of sherry". This should be a sweet sherry. You may wonder what size wine glass? Does it vary depending on the day you've had? Let me recommend 4 - 6 ounces of sherry. It is also unique to knead a cookie dough. Unique ingredients and techniques lead to a lovely tea cake.

1 cup unsalted butter	1 teaspoon vanilla extract
2 cup sugar	Wine glass of sherry
3 eggs	5 cups all-purpose flour, whisked

1. **Preheat oven to 350 degrees.**
2. Using a stand mixer, **cream butter and sugar** until fluffy, about 4 - 5 minutes.
3. **Add your eggs** one at a time. **Beat** after each addition.
4. **Add** the vanilla extract.
5. **Save 1 cup of flour** for the kneeding process. **Add 1/3** of the flour. Follow this with **half of the sherry**. **Add another third** of the flour. **Add the remaining sherry** and then flour.
6. **Remove the dough** from your mixing bowl on to a floured surface. **Knead** until the dough is smooth and well combined. If more flour is needed add by the tablespoon, making sure to incorporate it well.
7. **Roll thinly and cut** with a cookie cutter. This is a great opportunity to pick a shape that coordinates with the party or gathering where these tea cakes will be served.
8. **Cook** on a buttered or parchment paper lined cookie sheet for 10 - 14 minutes.
9. Makes about 100 tea cakes depending on size of your cookie cutter.

a Southern Legacy

grandmother's fruit cake cookies

I know that the words "fruit cake" may steer you away from this recipe.
Stop! This recipe is so much better than any fruit cake you ever encountered. These fruit cake cookies are soft and chewy, with a crunch from the nuts and are simply delightful to eat. I like that some of the techniques are different from how we make cookies today such as the beating of the egg white separate from the other ingredients. I have tried the "dump and go" method for these cookies. It doesn't work as well as the method listed below.
I've used this recipe in many classes and received raved reviews.
I hope your review is the same.

1/2 pound candied pineapple

1/2 pound dates

1/2 pound candied cherries (half red and half green)

1 cup pounds golden raisins

3 cups pecans, chopped

3 cups all-purpose flour, whisked

1 teaspoon cinnamon

1 teaspoon nutmeg

3 teaspoons baking soda

3 tablespoons milk

3/4 cup orange juice

1 cup light brown sugar

1 stick unsalted butter

4 eggs, separated

1. **Preheat oven to 350 degrees.**
2. **Dice all fruit and nuts.** The fruits are very sticky. Spray your knife with cooking spray to help reduce the stickiness on the blade.
3. In a large bowl, **combine spices and 1 cup flour. Add cut fruits and nuts** and **toss** to coat in the spiced flour mixture.
4. In stand mixer with whisk attachment, **beat the egg whites** until fluffy. Place them in a separate bowl until needed.
5. In the stand mixer, **cream butter and sugar** for 2- 3 minutes. **Add the other 2 cups of flour** to this mixture. **Beat in egg yolks.**
6. **Dissolve** baking soda in milk. **Add** the milk mixture to the flour mixture.
7. **Add** the nuts and fruits to the flour mixture. **Blend** well but gently.
8. **Fold in the egg white.** Be gentle.
9. Use a small ice cream scoop to **place cookies** on an ungreased baking sheet.
10. **Bake 20 minutes.** Allow to cool on the pan for 3 minutes.
11. Yields: 5 dozen

salted potatoes

Sometimes I say that recipes are not really a recipe but an assembly of items that make something. This is one of those dishes. You are basically boiling potatoes in a great deal of salt. I love serving this on a buffet or even as an appetizer. You really won't have to worry about having leftovers, ever! I have friends who are very upset when salted potatoes don't make an appearance at a gathering. Try not to disappoint your friends by leaving this off of your party food list.

2 pound bag small potatoes, like fingerlings or baby potatoes
1 cup salt
Sour Cream and grated Parmesan for dipping

1. In a large pot, **place potatoes. Cover with water** by at least 1 inch. Add salt.
2. **Boil** until potatoes are fork tender.
3. **Drain and serve**. Potatoes are good warm or room temperature. Do not make the day before and store in the refrigerator. The salt coating will be wet and not as appealing.
4. **Serve** by dipping potatoes in the sour cream and then the Parmesan cheese.

a Southern Legacy

pound cake cookies

The very first dessert that I ever published with professional pictures when I started Elizabeth's Edibles was this recipe. I topped the cookies with berries and almond whipped cream. It makes a grand summer dessert. Don't stop there. Dick and I love to take these on trips. My nieces like to decorate them. The dough can be frozen so you can always have cookies at a moment's notice.
Kathleen Howard Rambo this recipe is another winner that I love.

1 pound unsalted butter, no substitutions

2 cups sugar

4 egg yolks, beaten

5 cups all-purpose flour

2 teaspoons vanilla extract

1. In a mixer fitted with a metal whip, **cream together butter and sugar** until light in color.
2. **Add egg yolks slowly**.
3. Lower speed of mixer and **add flour**.
4. **Roll into 1 1/2" diameter cylinders** on waxed paper. **Wrap in plastic wrap and place in refrigerator** for 8 hours or overnight.
5. **Slice into rounds** and place on greased baking sheets.
6. **Bake in a 375 degree oven for 10 – 15 minutes.** The edges should be slightly browned, however the middle will still look slightly dough-like. Store with waxed paper between layers. Makes 36 cookies.

a Southern Legacy

oatmeal cookies

This is another recipe from the Hodges side of the family. If you are an oatmeal cookie lover, this is the recipe you have been searching for. The detail I saw when I first found this recipe is that it makes 10 dozen cookies. Now that would be baking for a crowd! Don't need 120 cookies? That is ok. All you have to do is cut everything in half in the ingredient list. You can freeze the dough and have oatmeal cookies anytime!

2 cups shortening

2 cups white sugar

2 cups brown sugar

4 eggs

2 cups nuts or coconut
(or one cup of each)

1 cup raisins (optional)

3 cups all-purpose flour

2 teaspoons baking soda

2 teaspoons salt

2 teaspoons vanilla extract

6 cups quick cooking oatmeal

1. **Preheat oven to 375 degrees.**
2. Using your standing mixer, **cream shortening and sugars** for 5 minutes.
3. **Add your eggs** one at a time.
4. In a medium bowl **whisk together flour, baking soda and salt.** Slowly **add this to the butter mixture**.
5. **Add the vanilla and the milk**. Slowly **add the** oatmeal, then nuts, coconut and finally the raisins.
6. Using a small ice cream scoop **place cookie dough** on a cookie sheet lined with parchment paper.
7. **Bake for 12 minutes.**
8. **Store** in airtight container.

wendy's pumpkin bread

In the Fall I am obsessed with pumpkin. Picking pumpkins has become a new thing in my life since I married Dick Weaver. We head to north Georgia and make a day out of finding the perfect pumpkins, picking apples and eating BBQ. I really enjoy pumpkin pie, pumpkin muffins and pumpkin soup. My sweet friend, Wendy Collins, shared this pumpkin bread recipe with me. It makes two large loaves. This allows you to keep one loaf and either share the other loaf or freeze it for later.

3 cups sugar

4 large eggs

2 teaspoons baking soda

2 teaspoons salt

2/3 cup water

1 teaspoon cinnamon

1 cup vegetable oil

15 ounce can pumpkin puree

1 teaspoon allspice

1 teaspoon nutmeg

3 1/2 cups all-purpose Flour

1 1/2 cups raisins or craisins

1. **Beat first 11 ingredients** on a low speed until blended.
2. **Stir in** raisins or craisins.
3. **Pour evenly** into 2 greased loaf pans.
4. **Bake at 350 degrees for 1 hour and 15 minutes.** Test with toothpick for doneness.
5. **Cool in pans for 10 minutes.** Remove from the pans and cool completely on wire racks.

a Southern Legacy

Just like a theatre production, creating a cookbook does not happen overnight. Nor does a cookbook happen just by the author. I decided to self-publish my first cookbook. After working decades in the arts, I have many wonderful contacts who could help me make my cookbook dream happen. I started to reach out to these friends and what you are holding in your hand right now is a result of my connections and their creativity, time and input.

I tell my culinary students all the time that we can look at our food all day but until we taste it we will never know if it is good or not. The same thing is true when you are writing recipes. They must be tested and critiqued. I'd like to thank those initial recipe testers who jumped in with both feet to read my words and cook my recipes. Thank you to Daniel Carne, Denise Richardson, Lynn Hadden, Laura Kjeidson, Leslie Page and Jill Rome. Putting your recipes out in front of the public for review is a daunting task. This group was so helpful, constructive and kind. I am grateful.

Once the recipes were written, they had to be edited. Believe me the old saying that you cannot edit your own work is so true. I found it very interesting to see what everyone caught and how they interpreted each word on the page. Without Dick Weaver, Carol Aebersold, Leslie Page and Jill Rome you might be ready a completely different book! My favorite repetitive comment from my editors is that they are so hungry after reading the recipes. These are the best words ever to a chef!

When prepared to write this cookbook, I asked my Facebook followers what they wanted in a go-to-cookbook. Overwhelmingly, they said that the finished shot of the recipe is the most important piece for them. My husband and I knew we had to find a great photographer who could take food photographs that would make you want to lick the page. Keith Goodwin, a neighbor and professional photographer, is a foodie's best friend. I practically cried the first day of shooting for this cookbook. I could not believe what I was seeing were my dishes. They all looked so fantastic.

There are certain people you meet in your life that you just know will always be in your life. When I started Elizabeth's Edibles 6 years ago I needed a logo for my business. There was only one person to contact. Holly Corin is a dear friend that I met in college. She is a fabulous artist and a true Southern girl herself. We worked together for years in the arts. She and her husband designed sets for my musicals. She has been there through so many highs and lows in my life. What I love most about Holly is that she knows what is in my head with only the briefest amount of information from me. She created the cover and handled all of the layout for this book. BRAVA! Thank you for bringing the visual life to my cookbook.

There are other individuals who listened, guided and held my hand at different points during this process. Thank you Steve McAbee for your social media guidance. I can't begin to thank my social media marketing intern, Kelly Griffin! She makes me look so good and makes sure that I am constantly in front of others. To my book mentors, Carol Aebersold and Holiday Miller, thank you for answering my questions and being honest.

There is no part of this book that would be possible without my family, after all they are part of the generations! My Mom tested recipes, interpreted handwriting and gave me valuable history lessons. My Dad found recipes I remembered but didn't have the actual recipe. My Aunt Sue cheered every moment of the process and gave me honest feedback. My daughter, Caroline, kept me from jumping off ledges when I wasn't sure I really have what it takes to be a cookbook author. Then my extended family checked on me regularly, said wow when I needed it and listened. What a blessing!

My final thank you is to my husband, Dick Weaver. He is my constant cheerleader. No one believes in me and fights harder to help me succeed than him. He has 'lived" this process with me; counseling, correcting, gently pushing, editing, tasting, shopping, driving, and talking me up to others every chance he gets. It is overwhelming at times to think about his deep love for me and his desire to see me succeed. I love you, Dick Weaver, with all of my heart.

Index

CPSIA information can be obtained
at www.ICGtesting.com
Printed in the USA
FSOW04n1844231017
40071FS